# GO SOLO

Contemporary Monologues for Young Actors

Edited by Matt Buchanan and Jonathan Dorf

www.youthplays.com
info@youthplays.com
424-703-5315

*Go Solo* © 2015 YouthPLAYS
All rights reserved. ISBN 978-1-62088-507-9.

**Caution:** These plays are fully protected under the copyright laws of the United States of America, Canada, the British Commonwealth and all other countries of the copyright union and are subject to royalty for all performances including but not limited to professional, amateur, charity and classroom whether admission is charged or presented free of charge.

**Reservation of Rights:** These plays are the property of their authors and all rights for their use are strictly reserved and must be licensed by their representative, YouthPLAYS. This prohibition of unauthorized professional and amateur stage presentations extends also to motion pictures, recitation, lecturing, public reading, radio broadcasting, television, video and the rights of adaptation or translation into non-English languages.

**Performance Licensing and Royalty Payments:** Amateur and stock performance rights are administered exclusively by YouthPLAYS. No amateur, stock or educational theatre groups or individuals may perform these plays without securing authorization and royalty arrangements in advance from YouthPLAYS. Required royalty fees for performing these plays are available online at www.YouthPLAYS.com. Royalty fees are subject to change without notice. Required royalties must be paid each time these plays are performed and may not be transferred to any other performance entity. All licensing requests and inquiries should be addressed to YouthPLAYS.

**Author Credit:** All groups or individuals receiving permission to produce these plays must give the author(s) credit in any and all advertisement and publicity relating to the production of this play. The author's billing must appear directly below the title on a separate line with no other accompanying written matter. The name of the author(s) must be at least 50% as large as the title of the play. No person or entity may receive larger or more prominent credit than that which is given to the author(s) and the name of the author(s) may not be abbreviated or otherwise altered from the form in which it appears in this Play.

**Publisher Attribution:** All programs, advertisements, flyers or other printed material must include the following notice:
    Produced by special arrangement with YouthPLAYS (www.youthplays.com).

**Prohibition of Unauthorized Copying:** Any unauthorized copying of this book or excerpts from this book, whether by photocopying, scanning, video recording or any other means, is strictly prohibited by law. This book may only be copied by licensed productions with the purchase of a photocopy license, or with explicit permission from YouthPLAYS.

**Trade Marks, Public Figures & Musical Works:** These plays may contain references to brand names or public figures. All references are intended only as parody or other legal means of expression. These plays may also contain suggestions for the performance of a musical work (either in part or in whole). YouthPLAYS has not obtained performing rights of these works unless explicitly noted. The direction of such works is only a playwright's suggestion, and the play producer should obtain such permissions on their own. The website for the U.S. copyright office is *http://www.copyright.gov*.

# List of Monologues

## FEMALE CHARACTERS

### Comic Monologues

Love (Awkwardly) (1) ..................................................................6
What the Well Dressed Girl is Wearing..........................7
Totally Okay, Right Now ........................................................8
Lipstick and Heroics ................................................................9
Grow Up, Girls..........................................................................10
Piñata Utopia ............................................................................12
4 A.M............................................................................................13
Gwen and Mary at Glenn Ross...........................................14
Herby Alice Counts Down to Yesterday (1) ................17
The Adventures of Rocky & Skye ....................................18
The Superhero Ultraferno ....................................................19

### Serious Monologues

Xtigone (1) ................................................................................21
The Ghost Moments (1)........................................................23
Dancing With Myself............................................................24
The Locker Next 2 Mine (1) ...............................................25
The Secret Garden ..................................................................26
Slow...............................................................................................27
Le Goalie .....................................................................................28
screens..........................................................................................30
What Happened at the Mud Puddle (1)..........................31
Annatude.....................................................................................32
Cupid and Psyche: An Internet Love Story .................34
Dear Chuck (1)..........................................................................35
Clay (1) ........................................................................................37
Secret Life Under the Stairs (1) .........................................39
What Happened at the Mud Puddle (2)..........................40
Blood, Sweat, and Cheers....................................................42

Uncertainty Theory .................................................................... 43
Girl Friend .................................................................................. 45
Warriors (1) ............................................................................... 47
What Comes Around... ............................................................ 48
Children of Hooverville ............................................................ 50
One Good Thing (1) ................................................................. 51
ESL ............................................................................................. 53
Lockdown (1) ............................................................................ 54
The Locker Next 2 Mine (2) .................................................... 56
An Actual Baby Person ............................................................ 57
Chiraptophobia ......................................................................... 59
Between Mars and Me .............................................................. 60
Lockdown (2) ............................................................................ 61

FEMALE OR MALE CHARACTERS

Dear Chuck (2) .......................................................................... 63
Snakes in a Lunchbox .............................................................. 65
My Little Brother ...................................................................... 66
Dear Chuck (3) .......................................................................... 68

MALE CHARACTERS

Comic Monologues

One Good Thing (2) ................................................................. 71
Love (Awkwardly) (2) .............................................................. 72
Creature Features (Modern Day Mutants) (1) ...................... 74
HKFN: The Abbreviated Adventures of Huckleberry Finn 75
The Baseball King ..................................................................... 77
Xtigone (2) ................................................................................. 78
Last Right Before the Void ...................................................... 81
Techies ....................................................................................... 82
Two Dudes from Daytona ....................................................... 84
The Ghost Moments (2) ........................................................... 86

**Serious Monologues**

| | |
|---|---|
| Clay (2) | 89 |
| The Grippe of October (1) | 91 |
| Rumors of Polar Bears (1) | 92 |
| Creature Features (Modern Day Mutants) (2) | 94 |
| Exposure | 95 |
| One Good Thing (3) | 97 |
| Sunset Johnson | 98 |
| Rumors of Polar Bears (2) | 100 |
| What Happened at the Mud Puddle (3) | 101 |
| Love (Awkwardly) (3) | 102 |
| Platform Nine | 104 |
| The Grippe of October (2) | 105 |
| War of the Buttons (1) | 106 |
| Warriors (2) | 108 |
| Herby Alice Counts Down To Yesterday (2) | 109 |
| The Locker Next 2 Mine (3) | 110 |
| Long Joan Silver | 111 |
| War of the Buttons (2) | 112 |
| Secret Life Under the Stairs (2) | 114 |
| Warriors (3) | 115 |
| Rumors of Polar Bears (3) | 116 |

Cover design by Daniel Rashid.

Front cover photo by Jonathan Dorf.

Rear cover photo: SteppingStone Theatre's production of *Roll of Thunder, Hear My Cry* by Ed Shockley (St. Paul, MN; photo by Dan Norman).

## Introduction

Monologues can be beautiful. They can transport a play and the audiences watching it to another place and time, offer special insights into characters and the journeys on which they find themselves, and change the rhythm of a play's "music." On a practical level, monologues are ideal for auditions and classroom work, and often used for a variety of competitions.

In this collection, you'll find more than six dozen monologues, all from plays we publish at YouthPLAYS. Within that context, you'll find a great deal of variety. We've tried to balance serious pieces with more comic ones, opportunities for female actors with ones for males, and shorter monologues with longer ones. The majority of the characters are teens, though some are pre-teens, making for a large group of age-appropriate, challenging and diverse choices for young actors ranging from middle school through university.

Want to learn more about the play from which each monologue comes? On our website (www.youthplays.com), you'll have access to a substantial free excerpt from each script. Just visit the site and search the play title. Want to read the entire play? Each is available for purchase in print or as a digital script.

And now...read on, and break a leg.

Matt Buchanan and Jonathan Dorf, Editors

Note: Some monologues in this book appear in slightly different form than in their parent plays. In some cases, interrupting lines may have been eliminated or reassigned, and occasionally a word has been changed for clarity out of context.

# FEMALE

## LOVE (AWKWARDLY) (1)
by John Rotondo and Maryann Carolan

Wendy, a high school junior, describes her embarrassing sex talk with her parents.

WENDY: When I was 10, my parents decided it was time to have "the talk." Actually, my mom decided and sort of ambushed my dad into it. I came down for breakfast on Sunday morning and my mom announced we were all going to have breakfast together. This was unusual since my mom usually had a slice of toast and a vitamin and my dad had coffee and cigarettes. As far as I knew, I was the only one who ever had "breakfast" in that house. When I sat down, my mom said "We need to talk about the birds and the bees." She's a euphemistic woman. My dad is more direct. He said, "Noreen, if we're going to talk about it, we're going to call it sex." I find that you can never burst into flames when you most need to. My mom was going on, euphemistically, and my dad was correcting her. "Wendy, men have a "boilerplate", and women have a persimmon." He didn't really say "boilerplate" and "persimmon" but you get the idea. My mom gets hung up on details. For some reason, she wanted to make absolutely sure I knew exactly what it took to make a baby. She kept repeating "The "squib" goes into the "mizzenmast." The "squib" goes into the "mizzenmast." The "squib" goes into the "mizzenmast." She said it 18 times. By the 19th time, I snapped. "I GOT the "mizzenmast!" And I ran out of the room, mortified. That was the last time anyone ever talked about "waffle irons" in my house again!

## WHAT THE WELL DRESSED GIRL IS WEARING
by Arthur M. Jolly

Teenaged Sandra has been helping her best friend choose an outfit for her date...with Jimmy, the guy Sandra yearns for.

**SANDRA:** Why would I be mad? Just 'cause it's a double date and my guy isn't going to be there 'cause I made him up, so it's just me and you and your date...Jimmy. Perfect, perfect Jimmy. And his dimples. *(Beat.)* I mean—it's Jimmy. He doesn't want to go out with me, he wants to go out with you. And he doesn't like me, even though—you know. I've been completely and utterly in love with him since second grade...and I left all those little presents on his desk, and hung around by his locker everyday, and I put a tent in his backyard and slept there with that Valentine's Day sign I made. I was there a week. He was at his uncle's. *(Beat.)* Then when the sign didn't work, I thought—you know. Bigger. Maybe he just couldn't read my writing, so I spent everything I had saved on a huge billboard that said—Jimmy, I love you, ask me to the spring formal! ...but I spent all my money on the billboard so I couldn't afford a ticket... I just watched through the window. It was raining. I stood there, in the rain, and watched you and Jimmy dancing. Together. You were staring into his eyes the whole time. Those beautiful, sparkling eyes—full of mystery, full of promise. Eyes you could lose yourself in. *(Beat.)* Then I got bit by a raccoon.

## TOTALLY OKAY, RIGHT NOW
by Madelyn Sergel

Lizzie, 13, has just learned that her talented but shy and conservative friend is thinking of auditioning for a television talent program.

**LIZZIE:** You know how sometimes, at first you hear an idea and you think it's awesome and then you think about it for a second? Well this is sort of like that. Alisha has a really awesome voice. But she never tries out for anything. She hates even having to read out loud in class. She was nauseous for three days before her Civilizations presentation. I mean she just isn't bossy or pushy or...ambitious at all. She sings for us, with a CD and stuff. But maybe...even if you have one part of being able to do a really cool thing...maybe you don't have all the parts to make it a career. She would never wear glitter shorts with the pockets hanging out. She won't even wear glitter nail polish when we're doing manicures at Megan's. And she can take it off before she goes home. If they had TV shows about superstar crafters, that is what Alisha should do. But...that's not the way stuff is. And another thing. Superstar. That is so weird! I mean, Kath loves, I mean LOVES this singer. You...older people won't know him...well... Okay. Look at him. Doesn't he look almost exactly like Guy? See? See what I mean? But Kath totally ignores him. Guy's not a celebrity but...well...he is **nice**. For a guy.

## LIPSTICK AND HEROICS
by Evan Baughfman

Kathleen, teens or 20s, offers her opinion while auditioning for a superheroine group.

**KATHLEEN:** No, the whole "you go, girl" thing. I'm not comfortable with that. I don't wanna be defined by my gender, you know? Why do I have to be labeled "girl" or "woman"? I'm a *person*. ...I love women. Love that I'm a woman. I just don't get why this group has to flaunt its "woman-ness." Why can't we be more subtle in our approach? No offense, Victory, but your costume—it's all, what-if-Wonder-Woman-had-a-garage-sale. It's tacky and it gives off this message that in order to be powerful you have to be some flying cheerleader who can punch through walls. We don't have to be dressed like this to be respected or taken seriously. Actually, the exact opposite is happening. We female super-people *aren't* respected or taken seriously. ...I just don't get the costumes. They say the wrong thing. What's wrong with a T-shirt and jeans?

# GROW UP, GIRLS
by Rex McGregor

Wendy, 16, a spoilt girl with a severe case of Peter Pan syndrome, has just discovered her governess, Nana, leaving with a suitcase. Nana is a woman wearing a full-body Newfoundland dog costume.

**WENDY:** Going somewhere?

*(Nana stops and hangs her head in shame.)*

Are you expecting a litter and keen to give birth without human intervention? Or have you got rabies and you're leaving us to avoid infecting the household? Help me out here. I'm trying to think of any reasonable justification for you sneaking away in the middle of the night. Do you need to go and nurse a dying relative in Newfoundland? If you can put a charitable spin on this exhibition of canine disloyalty, I'd love to hear it. You must admit it looks suspiciously as if you're deserting your post. But surely not. That would mean you're an ungrateful... I believe the correct word is bitch.

*(Nana expresses shock.)*

By the way, aren't you supposed to be on all fours?

*(Nana expresses resentment.)*

It's in the contract.

*(Nana reluctantly gets down on her hands and knees. Wendy pats a thigh, indicating, "Come." Nana doesn't budge.)*

Not very well trained, are you?

*(Nana reluctantly approaches. Wendy pats her affectionately.)*

Bad dog. You know I've got exams at the moment. You're meant to be protecting me from distractions, not causing them. Do I have to contact the agency?

*(Nana expresses anxiety.)*

All right, Nana. I'll let you off this once.

*(Nana nuzzles Wendy, expressing gratitude.)*

Now get back to work and we'll say no more about it.

*(Nana gives an exasperated huff.)*

Excuse me. Was that the obligatory cheerful bark?

## Piñata Utopia
by Christian Kiley

A young girl stops the guests at her birthday party from hitting Princess Piñata by delivering this speech, which has a touch of *Braveheart* in it.

**GIRL:** *(Throws herself in front of Princess:)* Stop, you freak show heathens! If we continue to ignore this atrocity, what are we? *(To the guests at the party:)* You want candy? *(Grabbing candy from her pockets:)* Here.

*(Girl throws candy around as the Children scurry for it.)*

This is what you want. Have it. But you will not beat and destroy my hero today, perfect in her imperfections. She will hang over our dining room table as a reminder of our imperfections and our desire to strive to be more civilized. We should see her when we eat to remind ourselves of the cannibalistic nature of society. Poetic license. I know what a cannibal is, Mother. *(To the crowd:)* As for the rest of you, ride your sugar high into some karaoke disaster of your favorite song. You will want to forget that song. But never forget this day.

## *4 A.M.*
book by Jonathan Dorf, music and lyrics by Alison Wood

Teenaged Frankie, a short-wave radio DJ, broadcasts from her bedroom. She has no idea whether her show has any listeners at all.

**FRANKIE:** This is Frankie telling you what's good and what's bad, so don't be sad, because I'm here to chase away those wee hour blues with my tell it like it is reviews. We'll be burning the way past midnight oil until this movie ends, and speaking of movies, the one everybody's talking about and you don't want to be left out... The Teenage Boy Played by a Twenty-Eight-Year-Old Actor Who Sulks and Wears Dark Earth-Toned Clothes Since the Death of His Mother Two Years Ago In a Drunk Driving Accident He Feels Responsible For and His Father's Absence Due to an All-Consuming Job Falls in Love with the Girl Everyone Thinks is Ugly But Has a Heart of Gold and Hidden Artistic Talents and They Develop an Unexplained Connection While They Fight Space Aliens Disguised as Terrorists and Seek the Treasure That Turns Out Not To Be What They Thought It Was But They Act Vulnerable as They Reveal Secrets and Save the World and the Ugly Girl Turns Out to be Hot Once They Give Her a Better Hairstyle and Color Coordinated Clothes and Remove the Makeup While They Come of Age and Learn a Valuable Lesson and Kiss as the Movie Ends Before Anything Else Can Go Wrong. Greatest movie ever. *(Beat.)* Not. But that song. Not that one. The other one. Music to my ears. *(Beat.)* Here on this show, we are not afraid to speak the truth—even if the phone lines light up with angry callers. Even if there are death threats. *(Beat.)* Even if nobody's listening at all.

## *Gwen and Mary at Glenn Ross*
by Robin Pond

Gwen, an ambitious, scheming pre-teen student, accosts her teacher, Mr. Johnston, in the school yard at lunch time, to lobby for inclusion in the group that will receive the enrichment math questions.

**GWEN:** Mister... Mister... Mister... Mister Johnston... Mister Johnston...wait...wait...wait. Mister... Mister... Mister Johnston... Mister Johnston...

I just...I just needed to ask...about the extra work. You're...you're giving it to Becky...to Becky. And she's okay... a sharp girl... She's okay. I get it.

(*Mr. Johnston starts to turn away. Gwen grabs at his arm.*)

No... no... wait... I need... we need to talk... I know it's lunch. I'm gonna go eat. We're all gonna eat. But first we gotta talk...you know...we gotta...about the extra work. Like...okay...I understand Becky. She's a regular on the honours board...a regular. But my name's always up there too. Right up near the top...right at the top...my name's always on the board. Or it was...it always was. And it can be again... It will be...I'm sure of it... It will be... One good test...just one...that's all it takes. I'm still the best...the tops...when it comes to math...any type of math. You know I am. You don't wanna waste the extra work on Mary...not on Mary. She's not gonna know what to do with it. And Georgie? You're giving it to Georgie...Mary and Georgie? Really? You'll give it to them...to Becky...to Mary and Georgie...a bunch of kids who've never been nearly as good at math...who wouldn't even know what to do with extra work...who'll just squander the opportunity...just not benefit from it. But I've shown...I've always shown...I've been tops... Last semester...semester before that...always... Just ask Mr. Murray, he'll tell you... Ask him... Always the top marks in math... I single-handedly brought up the class average...on last year's standardized test. It was me...me alone...putting our class above all the others in the state... That was me... You don't know about last year...of course you don't... You weren't the teacher last year, were you? Mr. Murray was... But I'm telling you...I'm telling you about last year...how I was the best...how I carried the whole class.

## GOLDEN LADDER

by Donna Spector

Teenaged Catherine, whose parents are from different religious traditions, has been struggling with her own religious identity. She has just had a fight with a Jewish friend.

**CATHERINE:** The end of the school year passed in a haze of unhappiness. Aaron was right: I was so defensive I'd squeezed my heart into a rock that hurt my chest whenever I breathed. I was tired of swearing and talking tough. I didn't want to be a Presbyterian any more. But I didn't want to be an atheist, because if there was a Hell I'd probably go there. And I didn't know how to be Jewish. I kept dreaming about the golden ladder Daddy talked about when I was little. I knew that was the name of the novel he'd been writing for years, and I wanted to read it. I thought maybe there were secret instructions for becoming wise, so I could climb that golden ladder right up to Heaven. But he wouldn't let me read it till it was finished. So I had no hope of figuring things out. Then one morning in the middle of summer I woke up and I knew what I had to do. The answer was so clear I started laughing, so I knew I was on the first step up that golden ladder. I had to become a Catholic!

## *HERBY ALICE COUNTS DOWN TO YESTERDAY (1)*
by Nicole B. Adkins

Clarissa, early to mid teens, is the lead reporter of the school newspaper and the portrait of perfection. She speaks to aspiring reporter Rose, who is not nearly as popular.

**CLARISSA:** *(To Camera Guy:)* Get this on camera, please. I want a witness. *(Beat.)* I'm not going to have the Times Daily Tribune Broadcast Blog and Live Journal Television and Interweb look like a bunch of yahoos. The media makes the story, Rose. Just like the historian writes the history. *(Beat.)* And let me be frank with you: the viewers make the ratings. *(Beat.)* Besides, we have to please the Powers-that-Be. The higher-ups. I promised. And I don't break my promises. *(Beat.)* Do you? *(Beat.)* Good. Now about the interview. Let's talk about portrayal. You know that our viewers have certain expectations. Disappointing our viewers equals bad. Happy viewers equals good. Laughing at others makes the viewers feel better about themselves, and gives them a united purpose...thus bringing the community together and equaling happy viewers. Happy viewers equal happy executives. Happy executives mean happy Clarissa. Which means Rose gets to be somebody. And isn't that what you want? What you've been working toward? *(Beat.)* Go get me that interview. And it better be splashy.

## THE ADVENTURES OF ROCKY & SKYE
by Kelly DuMar

It's picture day for middle schooler Ratani, who wants everything to be perfect.

**RATANI:** *(Confidently:)* Hi! Aren't you the same photographer as last year? Wow! I didn't think you'd be back after the incident with Todd Bright. Can you believe he wasn't even suspended? *(Posing:)* I love picture day! Not everybody does, but I do, because I come prepared. I remind all my friends, but nobody listens. It's like they just roll out of bed and say, oh, it's picture day, guess I better brush my teeth. Like it's too much hassle to pick an outfit the day before? Make sure it's clean? Comb your hair? *(Posing:)* My friend Rocky, he woke up with a big pimple right here — so he pretended he was sick, but the nurse sent him back to class just in time for pictures. I told him, don't worry — that's why they invented retouching! *(Posing:)* You have my form, right? I checked Package A+ Deluxe with the Misty Blue background — the gray would look really pukey with my dress, don't you think? *(Smoothing her dress with her hands:)* My father let me buy it even though my mother says I'll never wear it again. And these shoes — they weren't even on sale! He might not have told her about the shoes yet. *(Posing:)* What do you mean it's just a headshot? You're kidding! Wow, he's gonna be bummed. *(Posing:)* Are you sure you got a good one? Great! Well, I hope for your sake Todd Bright's out sick today. Bye!

## THE SUPERHERO ULTRAFERNO
by Don Zolidis

The Scarlet Witch, a superhero in her late teens or early 20s, is competing for the position of Sorcerer Supreme. This is part of her speech at the competition.

**SCARLET WITCH:** *(Confidently:)* Thank you. So all right— first of all—the guys around here are total losers, all right? So my friend Gina sets me up with her brother's friend, Tommy. Right? I don't know Tommy—I'm like, "Who's Tommy?" she's like, "He's nice." I'm like, "He sounds like a loser." Just 'cause of the name. I've never met a Tommy with a job. So he shows up for our *(air-quotes)* date. I'm putting date in quotes right now 'cause what was about to transpire does not really qualify for the word. Okay, let me describe Tommy. First of all I can smell Tommy when he is a block away—this cloud of cologne comes down the street, comes to my house, opens my door by itself, and punches me in the face. Tommy is orange. He's got enough gel in his hair to suspend a horse from a bridge. He's got a tattoo over the top of his chest that says "The Greatest." How do I know what it says? Because he's wearing a tank top. For a *date*. I'm thinking nice restaurant, I'm wearing heels, I went tanning that day—to look nice, you know? First thing he does, lifts up his shirt. Says, "Feel my abs."

I'm like, "No."

"Feel them."

"No."

"Feel them they're awesome."
"I'm not feeling your abs!"

"Wanda, I'm letting you touch me! Touch them, dang it! You

know you want to!"

"No!"

"Fine. You know what? This coulda been the best night of your life. You just ruined it."

We go to the gym. Let me repeat that in case you didn't hear me properly: WE GO TO THE GYM. Starts working out. I'm making small talk, you know.

"You got a job?"

"I'm working on it."

"So that's a no."

"Why you gotta be judgmental? First date. You're judgmental! You want to judge something? Judge this." He takes his shirt off. Starts flexing and looking in the mirror.

First thing I do—a little hex—Start his tattoo on fire. Not like a lot of fire, you know? I'm not cruel—but enough—he freaks out, flames are popping out of his chest. He's like, "Aaaaaaah! I'm burning! Help me!" Whatever. I'm like, "Stop, drop and roll"—he does that, cow falls on him. I don't have any control at this point. This 900-pound cow smashes through the ceiling, lands on him. Breaks a couple of his bones, whatever. He gets up, limping, still on fire, runs out into the street—"Aaaaaaah!" Gets run over by a car. Another car hits him. This is Jersey, there's a lot of traffic. Here comes this semi next.

In the hospital later I set him on fire again. Just cause.

Later he tweets about it—like, "That chick totally wanted me."

And that's when the airplane fell on him.

## *XTIGONE (1)*
by Nambi E. Kelley

Tigs, a girl in her late teens with a warrior's heart, is in cuffs, about to be buried alive for defying her uncle Marcellus.

**TIGS:** Blessed are they
Whose days are free of Sin.
No single soul can begin
Livin'
Who are steepled and people'd
In blood called Winnin'.

Poor Marcellus...

It's a lot of crazy in this world
There are the folks that love to hate and hate to love
Steady tryin' to tell you how to live from above
Takin' over startin' over cause it's the thrill of the kill
Killin' wo-man cause Marcellus da Man must hate mostly himself *and*
The Mama that be his homeland.
He destroyin' wetlands
And icelands and sand lands creatin' candy-less lands

He send my death to every coroner of the earth
To kill himself
So that he may reign and rain more dirt.

I am The Amazons of the Dahomey
Jamaica's Nyabinghi
The Queen called Nefertiti
Coretta
Rihanna
And Mama Obama's legacy

And if I stand still
I'm also Mamie Till

Not X'ed.
Not X'ed
Not X'ed —

## THE GHOST MOMENTS (1)
by Randy Wyatt

Charlene, late teens to early 20s, is dancing with her father, who has recently turned his life around.

**CHARLENE:** I was so close to slapping her, Daddy, I really was. Like she had any idea what we've been through. I think people like that feed off of tragedy, they really do. Like furry little spiders. Oh, and *then*, she goes "You're not gonna dance with him right there in front of everybody are you?" And I said "Damn *straight* I'm going to dance in front of everyone with him. He's my daddy, Mrs. Clemens, and I know you don't like him, and somehow you think that he owes us all just because he did drugs and drank and *gasp* *drove a motorcycle* when he was supposed to be going to your picnics and taking me to Sunday School, but you know what? We got our happy ending. He did the work, he sobered up, and now he's here. And just because he ain't jumping all over you to tell his stories in front of the whole ding-dang church doesn't mean anything except that he's done with the past, and so am I." And then I left her there without saying another word, and her mouth was so wide open I was thinking she could catch flies. The nerve of her.

You know what, Daddy? It was right then that I thought to myself "Charlene, you won. You crossed the finish line, and you did it together. And we got each other as the prize." And Daddy, you are my prize. There is no one I would rather be dancing with right now on the face of this earth than you. And you know what? You're still no better at it than you were back when you were stone drunk.

## *Dancing With Myself*
by Leanne Griffin

Goth Girl, a teen determined to be different but beginning to question her choices, speaks first to her controlling boyfriend on the phone and then to the audience, about her decision to attend a school dance.

**GOTH GIRL:** Hello? Hello! I told you...I'm at the dance! ... I know. I know! It's just... With my friend. My friend! ... Yes, I know you think it's a cliché. Yes, I know you told me not to go but... Stop telling me what to do! No. I'm staying!

*(The other girls back away and stand around her, like the bars of a cage.)*

Fine then! Hello? Hello?

*(She hangs up. The lights come up to full. The other girls silently cross by Goth Girl. They meld into the darkness, lying, or sitting on the floor. Goth Girl stares straight ahead, listening to the music. She slowly hugs herself, and covers her face with her hands, then looks up again and takes off her skull cap.)*

I was feeling so small and apart, like society had me trapped in a cage. I thought he was the key to it all. And then he opened the door to my heart and for a while it felt like everything was perfect. That I was perfect. In the beginning he made me feel so unique, so special, so amazing. He made me feel...absolutely free. But then things changed. It was like he couldn't stand to just let me be, he had to control me and change me, and he made this big deal about not wanting me to conform but you know he just made me conform to him. And now...he's just a different cage.

## THE LOCKER NEXT 2 MINE (1)
by Jonathan Dorf

Luna, a teenager, stands alone on stage and speaks.

**LUNA:** Pluto was officially discovered in 1930. It became the ninth planet, and the farthest from the sun. What a lot of people don't know—no, what pretty much everybody doesn't know, is that its orbit crosses Neptune's, the eighth planet, but the two planets don't ever come close to each other. *(Beat.)* So Pluto's always been this lonely little planet, and it's cold. Really, really cold. Like negative 230 degrees Celsius cold. People couldn't live there. *(Beat.)* I'm pretty sure most people don't spend a lot of time thinking about Pluto. Why would you? Pluto doesn't get you an A in English or pay your car insurance or keep your mom from aiming a half full coffee mug at your dad's head on the last night you pretended you had a functional family. *(Beat.)* But then it happened. In 2006, Pluto got demoted. One day it's a planet, and the next day it's not. They come up with this new category: a dwarf planet. Sure, Pluto, you're separate but equal. Right. And finally people take notice. Harvard students stage a sit-in at University Hall, in Berkeley they burn a revised map of the solar system and protestors take to the streets of Manhattan to stand up for Pluto. *(Beat.)* I made that last part up. Outside of a few astronomers, nobody really cared, and after a few weeks, people stopped talking about it. Nobody ever stands up for the Plutos of the universe. At least not in my universe. *(Beat.)* Our school has a Pluto problem.

## THE SECRET GARDEN
by Isabella Russell-Ides

Mary Lennox, 14, a newly orphaned English girl raised in India, has just met her cousin Colin Craven in the English country house to which she has moved.

**MARY:** Your eyes are beautiful. It's odd—when I try to remember Mother's face, it's like looking in a foggy mirror. And when I think of my Ayah the fog clears. That's pathetic, don't you think? To remember a servant and not your own mother. *(Beat.)* But this portrait is so like. It brings her back, as if Mother were right here—seated at her dressing table. I can almost hear the ghostly orchestra rehearsing in the ballroom.

Mother loved to dance. She had so many beautiful gowns. I used to sneak into her room and study her reflection in the looking glass. I loved to see our faces in the mirror, side by side. Sometimes she'd let me try on one of her pretty jewels. "Stop chattering at me like a monkey. Come, give us a kiss." And I would go and kiss the air, next to her cheek.

She was always getting ready to leave.

After everyone died, I went back to the looking glass to see if I could make her appear. There was a camellia dying in a bowl of water. I was so thirsty, I drank the water.

Her name was Camellia. She loved to pin flowers in her hair.

## SLOW

by Keegon Schuett

Teenaged Lizzie loses it talking to Marsha, a popular girl she thinks is moving in on her boyfriend.

**LIZZY:** I hate you! I hate you!

Let me have some peace and quiet, you bike and boy stealing bimbo. You know what I hate most about you? People want you to succeed. People want you to do well and if that means trampling over the little people then so be it. Speaking of trampling all over people...nice rhinoplasty, you rhino. Everyone knows about it. It's not a secret. If anything, it's just sad that you change your face. Cut it apart and paste it back together and everyone treats you even better. Encouraging you.

And your skin! It glistens. I hate it...are you even real? In photographs you look plastic. You know what I think about every time I take your picture? I think "Maybe photos do steal a piece of the soul. I can't see one behind those Barbie eyes." You smile your empty smile and behind your eyes is nothing. Do you even have a soul? Do you care? You're cold and cruel and I hate you. I hate you! I hate you!

## *Le Goalie*
by Nelson Yu

Shelly, 12, is a hockey forward. She is alone on stage, speaking about her friend, another hockey player.

**SHELLY:** So I have this French friend, Fabrice. He's not really French, he's from Quebec... He's a real piece of work. *(As if talking to somebody who doesn't understand:)* Meaning, he's kinda hard to convince to do the right thing. He's stubborn. I mean, I'm a girl, but I'm like the best forward in the whole league. And Fabrice is the best goalie. We made each other. *(Pause.)* Now you're probably asking...what is a girl doing in a boys' hockey league? Pffft. I'm so much better than most of them—they had to let me play. Everybody loves a winner, right? Anyways, Fabrice thinks he's better than Patrick Roy or some other French goalie. Whatever. I let him think that because goalies are hard to find—nobody wants pucks slapped into their face. *(Shrugging:)* And I needed somebody to practice with.

*(Shelly flashes back to the previous game against Fabrice.)*

So last game. Our team needed to beat Fabrice's stupid team to head to the finals. The score was tied four-four. I hadn't scored since Fabrice's team was double and triple teaming me. But I knew it would eventually happen. I always score. Scouts were at the game, you know. I was going to get drafted high to a good Bantam team, I was certain...if Fabrice hadn't ruined it for me.

*(Shelly slaps a puck — then shakes her head at the result.)*

He knew I liked going five hole when the puck was wobbling. He was lucky I couldn't get a clean shot! Cuz I always score on him. His weakness is high blocker side. I always go there when I can. *(Approaching Fabrice:)* Then to make it worse, he slashes me afterwards.

*(Shelly acts as if she's been hacked on the calf.)*

So I had to slash him back.

*(Shelly responds by "two-handed slashing" Fabrice.)*

Then I hear *(As the referee:)* Two minutes for unsportsmanlike conduct. *(As herself:)* What? He slashed me first! *(As the referee:)* Two minutes in the sin bin, young lady. *(As herself:)* I swear I heard his teammates tell Fabrice to slash me earlier. His team is so annoying—they say stuff like "How's your boyfriend?" or "Are you gonna go home and cry if I trip you?" His coach is constantly complaining about me and the refs never call penalty when I'm hooked. Everybody hates me!... And because of my penalty, they score! And we lose!

## SCREENS

by Jessica McGettrick

Alex, female, a high school freshman who has been a target of bullying behavior for years, has had enough of it.

**ALEX:** I'm so sick of this. I'm SO done. Every day goes so fast. I can't keep up. At school I don't know what to say to anyone. So many other people have it just right. Laura has just the right thing to say at just the right time. Laura always gets the biggest laughs from everyone, even teachers. I can be funny, I just have to think about it a little longer. How does she DO it? It's like she has a script, all of them do, and I have to improvise. Like, one day, when our biology teacher made a really corny joke, suddenly it came to me, like a "pop," like a static electricity shock—I thought of the funniest thing to say back, and I tried to say it out loud, but it was just really quiet, and only Laura could hear me. She looks over, and says, "Alex, seriously? Grow up." Then SHE raises her hand, and says exactly what I just said, and everyone laughed their heads off. It's not fair, but whatever. I guess I am getting used to it. *(Beat.)* That's not true. I'm not used to it at all.

## *What Happened at the Mud Puddle (1)*
by Tara Meddaugh

Amanda, middle or early high school and new, has been invited to a popular but mean girl's yacht party.

**AMANDA:** I wanted to go to Chloe's party. I did. She's kinda nice, and she's helped me open my locker a few times before. And she didn't make a big deal about it either. She said it happens to everyone, so don't worry, and smiled at me. Taylor's really pretty, I guess, and people seem to wonder what she thinks about a lot of things, but I don't like Taylor. I moved here in December and even though Mrs. Fields told her to help me find my way around, she didn't. But she didn't just ignore me, which would have been, I don't know, not really nice either. But she actually, I don't know, tricked me and stuff. She told me I had to pay the lunch lady in all pennies, or else I couldn't buy lunch, so she made me sit by the windows by myself, and I was starving that first day. And the next day, when I collected all the pennies in my mom's purse and in the car, and went to pay the lunch lady, she was really annoyed with me, and kind of yelled at me in front of the other kids and said, "How am I supposed to count all these pennies with a line of kids behind you?" And she made me wait until all the other kids had their lunch and then counted the pennies and I barely had time to eat that day. And when I sat down, Taylor had told everyone how poor I was that I only had pennies for lunch. I know I shouldn't have believed her. But. I don't know. I usually just believe people. Because, why would they lie? *(Pause.)* Chloe and Taylor usually sat next to each other at lunch, but I noticed Chloe sat somewhere else that day. I should have gone to her party. But Taylor asked me. To go to her party. *(Pause.)* And that's why I went.

## ANNATUDE

by Kenyon Brown

Anna, 15, is in chemotherapy for lymphoma. Her mother has taken her on a "vacation from cancer" and she's been texting her best friend, Kiele, another girl in chemo.

**ANNA:** On the last day, after we checked into the hotel, Mom totally surprised me when she said I could invite Kiele to spend the night with me if I wanted. Sweet! Of course I texted Kiele right away. "Hotel is awesome. Our own room. Please say you will come." I was even wearing the fireworks scarf Kiele gave me. I waited and waited and waited, but she didn't text me back. "Maybe she wants to be by herself," Mom said. Did Kiele need a break from me, too?

You never know when you'll meet someone who'll suddenly change your life. Like the time I walked into study hall, and sitting there was this girl.

"My name's Kiele," she said.

"I'm Anna," I said.

And just like that Annie was over. I was Anna. And we became the Hurl Girls.

This one time we're in study hall, and I tell Kiele about the ugly duckling-moth-rose bud metaphors my Mom uses to cheer me up. I ask Kiele if her Mom uses the same lame comparisons. "More lame," Kiele says. "Cinderella, Sleeping Beauty, and Snow White. Like some prince is going to kiss me, and the cancer will be gone."

No more cancer. NMC. "Kiele," I ask. "What if the prince never finds Cinderella's shoe? And she's stuck at home with her gross stepmother and stepsisters? Or what if Prince Charming can't wake up Sleeping Beauty? Or what if the prince kisses Snow White, but it turns out he's not her true love, so the spell is never broken?"

"Exactly," Kiele says. "Somehow the endings have to change, and we have to save ourselves."

Rereading the texts we've sent each other, I'm trying to figure out what I said, or what I didn't say or should have said, or what Kiele thought I said, that's made her so mad at me. She hasn't texted me for a long time. Did I say something I shouldn't? What did I do wrong?

We've never had a fight, if this is a fight. Mostly we agree on stuff. It's like we know what the other is thinking. We know what the other is feeling. We really are like the PT. By calculating two fix points—here's me and there's Kiele—and then factoring in cancer as the third fixed object, we're like this triangle. We're a lot alike, but we're still different. Since we tell each other like practically everything, and share so much, we just know what the other is going through. But maybe I don't really know Kiele like I think I do.

*(She reads text on cellphone.)*

Kiele's in the intensive care unit—ICU—what? Her mom's been texting me from the hospital. Kiele has this infection. The cancer...has come back. How come Kiele didn't text me? I have to find out from her mom? I'm here, Kiele's there. What do I do? I don't know what to do.

IT'S SO NOT FAIR!!!

We pinky swore to get better together. I'm getting better. Kiele has to get better. She has to.

## CUPID AND PSYCHE: AN INTERNET LOVE STORY
by Maria Hernandez, Emma Rosecan and Alexis Stickovitch

Teenaged Izzy, a little tomboy, a little girly, a hopeless romantic, records a video blog.

**IZZY:** ...Homecoming isn't just one of those things you invite people to... But you don't want to go alone. Especially when all my friends have dates; annoying, but cute nonetheless. I don't know why guys don't like me. Everyone says I'm pretty, but apparently that's not enough. You have to be smart like Reed, or outgoing like Olivia. They never have trouble finding dates for the dance, not that they have to worry about that anymore. It really, really bothers me that— *(Beat.)* Never mind. *(Beat.)* On the flip flop, today in Latin class we finally got to mythology. We started with my favorite. The story of Cupid and Psyche. You know, Psyche was the last of her sisters to get a boyfriend too. Everyone agreed she was, in fact, the prettiest, but all her suitors were too intimidated to talk to her. It got to the point where her desperate parents went to the Oracle to see if she would ever get married. The Oracle told her parents to leave her on the side of the mountain and her husband would find her there and take her with him. And he did. And everything was awesome, except for the fact that Psyche's husband never let her see what he looked like. This didn't bother her, but her sisters convinced her looks are everything. So she decided one night to turn on the lights. And like that he was gone. He was there just long enough for her to see that he was the gorgeous god Cupid. *(She leans forward to turn off the camera:)* If I ever had someone that loved me like that, I'd never turn the lights on.

*(She turns camera off.)*

## DEAR CHUCK (1)
by Jonathan Dorf

A teen alone on stage isn't sure how to feel about a classmate with racist ideas.

**GIRL:** My grandma had numbers on her arm. She was really little—she had a hat that she wore every Saturday that was so big she disappeared in it—which made the numbers seem like they took up half her arm. They didn't—that was in my head—and she never said much about them. Only once, and that was just for five minutes one day when it was raining and I was staring. *(Beat.)* The boy in my math class has a swastika on his arm, but he loves numbers and what he can do with them, especially subtraction. He used to have wavy blonde hair, almost down to his shoulders, but then he subtracted it. He used to wear all these crazy colors like he was Bob Marley or something, but then he subtracted them. He used to walk me home, and my mom would make him stay and eat sandwiches, 'cause his parents were never home, but six months ago he subtracted me and the rest of his old friends and then he subtracted his name and became the boy in my math class. *(Beat.)* He doesn't just subtract. The boy in my math class adds too. He adds new friends that keep their swastikas covered under long undershirts, and he adds lots of words he learns on the internet, words like White Power and racial purity and the Big Lie and the Zionist Conspiracy. He says the sandwiches my mom used to make him were filled with dog food, and she was trying to poison him. *(Beat.)* We all have to teach a math lesson this year. Yesterday was his. He gets up, and he takes the chalk, and he goes to the board. He writes six million, and then he subtracts six million from it. And he's smiling and says zero is the answer. The teacher asks what the question is, and he says "six million is the number of Jews they say died in Europe between 1939 and 1945. Six million is the number the Jews made up. Zero is the number that really died. Not countin' natural causes or whatever." And the boy in my math class keeps smiling, like it's a joke, but he's not joking. *(Beat.)* And at that moment I want to subtract him. Not just subtract him from my class or from my school, but from the world. He's 16 years old, and he's got that smile I want to rip off his face. If he died I wouldn't care. Just let a car subtract him one night crossing the street or a bullet or cancer or just let somebody subtract his air until he can't breathe anymore. *(Beat.)* But then I remember my grandma and how she lived with the numbers she wanted to subtract. And I remember those five minutes in the rain when I asked about them, and if they still hurt. She said—real quiet, so my father wouldn't hear—"I wish they weren't there, but some things we just have to live with. Or live through."

## CLAY (1)
by Carol S. Lashof

Zeta, a high school junior, describes a different kind of peer pressure.

ZETA: Of course I cheat. Listen. I'm taking AP Comp, AP American History, AP Bio—there's like three hours of homework every night for just that one class, Honors Math Analysis, French—only third-year French, because I took Spanish in middle school, then I switched to French in high school because that's what all the other high-end kids were taking. Or Latin. Or both.

Junior year. That's what the colleges really look at, you know.
If I was one of the seriously smart kids, I would've taken Geometry in eighth grade, so I'd be in Calculus by now. And I'd be in fourth year French. And Latin. For instance, there's a girl on my crew team, Sophie Janowitz, she's only a sophomore, and she's first violinist in the orchestra, but she's in most of my classes. So I'm behind.

I don't cheat in Bio or History because I actually need to learn the material in those classes, so I can pass the AP exams. But if I wrote every English paper from scratch and never snuck a cheat sheet into a French exam, I would just die. The subjunctive? I mean seriously, what is the subjunctive? Truly, I have no idea.

Don't warn me about getting caught. I won't get caught. You only get caught if what you write yourself is bad and what you steal is good. But my work is fine.

I just don't have time to do it.

People say it's pushy parents who are to blame for kids like me taking too many AP classes and getting pneumonia. Or having a nervous breakdown. Or both. Because we're up 'til 1:00 in the morning doing homework and taking Adderall to stay awake 'cause we've been up since 4:30 in the morning doing Crew—if you want to go to an Ivy League, or any school that counts actually, any school that anybody's ever heard of—you'd better do either Crew or Lacrosse, and Crew doesn't require a tryout, just showing up. So I do Crew.

But it's not pushy parents. At least, not my parents. Actually, my mom tries to tell me not to do so much. But she doesn't understand. When she was my age, you could get into a good college with a 3.5 GPA and 1300, maybe even 1200, on the SATs. Can you imagine?

Also, I'm taking ceramics. I love being in that room—and just breathing. How could anyone not love the smell of clay?

Most people, when they talk about peer pressure, they mean pressure to do drugs and skip school and have sex. But that's not the pressure I feel. The pressure I feel is the pressure of all those other people like me, but better than me, about to graduate from high school and apply to college and it seems like they've all done these amazing things, like swum in the Olympics—swam?—or won the National Science Fair. Or both. And me, what have I done?

Maybe I could be a potter. Throw pots for a living. Does anyone actually do that?

## SECRET LIFE UNDER THE STAIRS (1)
by Kris Knutsen

Field, pre-teen or early teens, finishes reading what she's just written in her journal.

**FIELD:** I danced beneath your secret heights
A peak no one could see
I slew the boys
To be alone
with secret books
for me.
Digging a tunnel I flew to the sky
Freezing air a fire inside
but alone
with me
and just a book
is... *(Beat.)* Not much fun. *(Beat.)* The advanced class at school gets to study French and go on field trips to museums. Even though they're older, they feel more like me. We can't really afford the trips anyway. Instead I get a library card to check out books for free, and mom works extra hard so Catch can play baseball and have his own uniform. And I borrow distant places to travel on a page. *(Beat.)* Someday I'll go for real, you know? Take field trips of my own. *(Beat. Looking offstage:)* I could race, too, you know. They just get mad when I beat them.

*(Field leaves, following the boys.)*

## *What Happened at the Mud Puddle* (2)
by Tara Meddaugh

Ronni, middle or early high school, is at an extravagant yacht party her classmate, Taylor, has thrown. Taylor has been increasingly rude to her guests and Ronni has been noticing.

**RONNI:** I couldn't believe it when Jasmine first left. It's one thing for the boys—but one of her girls? To leave? I was, like, high-fiving her in my head though. Taylor was totally moving in on her guy. But when Taylor sees her leave—'cause she's watching, you know. She doesn't really care about the Lego Guy—Tom. When she sees her leave, she starts to lose it. She pulls Tom with her, but she's following Jasmine and swearing and calling her all sorts of names. And Tom totally doesn't get it. He's like a scarecrow or something. He's just standing there. I think he tried to get his hand free for a minute, but she just put her whole arm around him then. So I go to them and sort of release Tom and bring Taylor to the french fry bar—you know, like, a dozen different things to dip them in? Taylor won't eat them in front of anyone, but she loves them. So do I. That's why she had them there. So I give her a plate and tell her to relax. But you know, I don't know what I'm thinking. She's clearly not going to relax. So she throws the plate and the fries at me and says I'm in with Jasmine, and I'm like—"you know I'm in with Jasmine. I'm in with all my girls. So?" And she's like, "You're a traitor! Just like Chloe!" and I'm like, "What? I'm in with you too, Taylor!" But she's freakin' out. You know. She's screaming and pointing at me. So I just back up. I just back up and say, "You're totally being a psycho, and I warned you not to be a psycho." But you can't reason with her when she's in psycho-mode. What's the point? So the boat hasn't left. And I pity anyone on it if it does leave. But I just walk. She's yelling after me, "Yeah, you walk the plank, Ronni! You walk it!" and I'm like—"you know I'm gonna walk it like a runway, girl." So I do.

## BLOOD, SWEAT, AND CHEERS
by Kaci Beeler and Amy Gentry

Competitive cheerleader June Davis, 17, explains her struggles with perfection to her good friend James after he discovers a mean prank she pulled on a fellow cheerleader, Kennedy Campbell.

**JUNE:** I busted my tumbling at Nationals. That means I screwed up. It wasn't bad, it didn't cost us the Worlds bid, but I started to like, obsess over my performance. My cardio time, my calorie intake, every second of training had to count. It just made me start to hate myself. Like, if I wasn't pushing myself as hard as I could, every single day, it wasn't good enough. And if it wasn't good enough, then *I* wasn't good enough. You don't know what it's like, James. Having everyone expect you to be perfect all the time. If you're not the best, you're not going to win, and if you're not winning, you're a loser.

Anyway, it's not like I'm trying to excuse what I did. It was awful, I regretted it as soon as it happened. I'm just trying to explain. Kennedy is like the worst side of me, James. She's the me I could see myself becoming when I was in Austin Cheer Depot the first time, and I hated her. She's afraid all the time, and it makes her act horrible! *(Beat.)* I just—I didn't want that girl to be me. I wanted to show everybody that I'm different.

## UNCERTAINTY THEORY
by Maura Campbell

Sam delivers her high school graduation speech after the recent death of her best friend, Andrew.

**SAM:** Mr. Channing, honored guests, families and friends, and members of the Class of 2---. I began writing my speech right after Christmas. I like to be prepared. And I gave it to my English teacher who gave it to my history teacher. They made a few suggestions. I took them. I'm pretty good at taking suggestions. I'm pretty good at being pretty good. I like to plan, you see. I like to know what's going to happen.

When I moved here in the third grade the first person I met was Andrew Conley. He was obsessed with *Star Trek*. We used to argue for hours about whether the aliens were real or not. I mean, even in the third grade I knew it was only television. And it was repeats! I told him it happened years ago anyway so even if it was real it didn't matter because all those aliens must be dead by now. And he'd say, you've got brains, but you don't know everything. Then one day—maybe in the seventh grade—Andrew was sent home because he wouldn't take off his hat. He said he was growing antennae and he didn't want the teacher to see. He said she wouldn't understand. So the next day he came to school and I said, where are the antennae? Huh? And he said they're there. But now they're invisible. And I said, well, I should be able to feel them, right? Maybe they're invisible, but I should be able to feel them... So he took my hand. And he put it over his head. And there was something there. I have to remember that. I have to remember that every day. Something can be invisible but that doesn't mean it isn't there. I used to think uncertainty was the worst thing in the world. Now I think it's what keeps us looking up instead of away. Andrew—wherever you are—we'll see you soon. I'm certain.

## GIRL FRIEND
by Steve Lambert

Fiona, 17, stands before the grave of a friend at night and speaks to him. She wears casual clothes but has made an effort to look her best. She is underdressed for the weather and is visibly cold.

**FIONA:** Hiya.

How's it going?

Sorry about the get-up. It's just, last time I climbed over't railings, I tore me best coat.

Should be having my tea now. Do you miss 'avin' tea?

I know I said I'd bring flowers this time, but I thought it might upset Louise or your mam. Especially your mam. I followed her here last Sunday — she looked a right state. Still, she's lost loads of weight since you died, so, swings and roundabouts, eh?

She just needs to tidy herself up. Your Louise could help her with that.

Remember how windy it was at your funeral? Well, obviously, you don't, cos you weren't there. Well, you were there, but you know what I mean.

But this gale comes out of nowhere. And your mam, who wasn't lookin' so hot to start with, ends up looking like a bleedin' scarecrow.

But your Louise, not a hair out of place. I know she used enough lacquer to destroy the ozone layer, but even so.

She really looked the part. In that lovely black coat. Dabbing her eye with that hanky, all dainty like.

I'm not saying Louise wasn't upset an' that. But she was the Grieving Girlfriend and made sure everyone knew it.

You never told her about me, did you? Not that there was much to tell, from your point of view. But there was from mine. And you knew it. And you liked that, didn't you?

Remember when I found your address book?

I'm on checkout, never seen you before, and you're asking if there's a box you can put your shopping in. And I'm saying, sorry, you can't have one. Because Barry, the new manager, reckons they're a fire hazard.

So you looks at me, with them big dark eyes, and you say:

*Well, Barry's quite right. So many fires do start that way. You can scarcely open a paper without reading about some supermarket incinerated in a cardboard box-related fire tragedy. In fact, you can hardly walk through a shopping precinct without encountering some human torch that's staggered out of Tesco's.*

And then you dropped it. Your address book. When you took out your wallet. You didn't notice and I didn't say anything.

All them girls' names. Which made me think, with you being so pale and interesting, that you might be a poof. But I knew you weren't by the way you looked at me. Not that you fancied me. But when boys look at girls to see if there's any bit of her worth looking at.

Your address book had your address in it. So did mine, but only to make up the numbers. I phoned you up. Remember? So I could give it back.

*Meet me under the town hall clock tomorrow at six,* you say. Bloody cheek.

## WARRIORS (1)
by Hayley Lawson-Smith

Maddie, 12-14, writes in her diary, sorting out her emotions as she reveals that her older brother lies in a hospital, in a coma.

**MADDIE:** 22nd August, 2014. Dear Diary. See that hospital there? My brother is in that hospital. He'd be so embarrassed if he knew he was in there. But he doesn't know. He can't know. Peter isn't awake. Peter hasn't woken up since the ambulance brought him in. That was three weeks ago. The doctors said he'd been in the water too long... I haven't been to school the whole time. Mom and Dad haven't noticed. I don't think they'd care, anyway. It's weird to think that a little while ago, they were arguing about stupid things like who took the remote control. Now their fights aren't funny. They're scary. Dad says Mom needs to...let Peter go, that it isn't fair, that Peter...that Peter wouldn't want to be kept...like that. And Mom keeps yelling at Dad, "How could you let him swim alone? How could you let him swim alone?" Even though Peter always swims alone, he loves to swim and he never gets into trouble. *(Pause.)* Dear diary. I'm frightened. *(Pause.)* 24th August, 2014. Dear diary. I hate that my brain keeps coming up with stupid thoughts. Today I realized that rip is spelled R.I.P. I laughed. I'm such an idiot. I've come to visit Peter. Mom says I shouldn't visit him alone, that it's too...I don't care what she thinks. I want to see my brother. He needs to hear the sports results.

## *What Comes Around...*
by Tom Smith

Mandy, mid to late teens, is talking to Zack, same age and totally engaged by his computer or listening to music, in a coffee house.

**MANDY:** I wonder if you remember me from fifth grade.

I wonder if you even know my name.

Tech-boy? Zack? Hey, Tech-boy?

You're kinda cute. If you'd ever look up from that screen.

Maybe I should start a website and then you can read all about me. Mandy Conn: virtual screw-up. Frankly, it would be much better to be a screw-up online than it is in real-life. Online, you can't see your mom's disappointment.

I bet you want to know, don't you? I can tell. Well, then, yeah: the rumor is true... I bought a gun.

It feels good to tell someone that.

The nice thing about having a gun is that people aren't ignoring me now. In fact, next to being Homecoming Queen or Valedictorian, being the weird freak with a gun gets you all sorts of respect. People are nice to me now. No one is writing bad things about me anymore. No one makes rude comments as I walk by.

But the funny thing is...I wouldn't ever hurt anybody. Everyone's so worried that I'm gonna go all crazy and shoot up the school. But how much damage can I really do with a handgun? Besides, if I kill people then everyone will have a reason to hate me so much.

My plan is so much better. I mean, why kill other people when I can just off myself? Guilt lasts longer than revenge. Guilt lasts forever. Like a movie.

I can just see my mom's face. My teachers. People at school. You. Heck, it'll be especially bad for you, because you'll be thinking "I just sat with her at The Bean. She was drinking coffee at my table. And I never even acknowledged her existence." Boy, it sucks to be you right now, Tech-boy!

I'll tell you what. I like you. I'll give you a chance to say something to me. To acknowledge me. To see me. To give me a reason not to kill myself. I'll even give you a little help.

*(She waves to Zack. He sees her and ignores her.)*

## CHILDREN OF HOOVERVILLE
by Hollie Michaels

In Dust Bowl Era Middle America, Vivian, 14, confronts Elsie for having abandoned her and her sisters on Route 66, instead of waiting for Vivian's father to come back.

**VIVIAN:** What's the matter with me? With me? You're the one that left me and my sisters stranded! We had no food, no water! We walked for miles after waiting. Nobody ever came back for us. You could have taken us with you. Was that furniture worth more than our lives?

*(Elsie tries to speak but doesn't.)*

Some people passed. One offered us a ride but could only take one of us. So we kept on walking until our heels bled. And then finally we got to that great big mountain and some folks said we could ride with them if we helped carry their furniture up the side of the mountain by foot. So we did and they nearly drove off but we jumped on and held on for dear life. Just went from caravan to caravan like beggars! Then, a few towns from here, we saw him, our Pa. Said he thought you all would look after us. He didn't have much else to say after that.

## ONE GOOD THING (1)
by Don Zolidis

Erynne, 17, a troubled punk girl, talks to her boyfriend, Nemo.

**ERYNNE**: When I was 12, my older sister Dierdre was killed in a car accident. It wasn't exactly an accident. Her and her friends were car surfing, which is where one kid gets on top of the car and either stands up or just holds on as they drive around like crazy. And so they were doing this in the park, and I guess some of her friends had gone already—and I never really knew if she was drunk or not while she was doing this, but I guess she probably was, anyway, they went around a corner and she rolled off and hit her head on the pavement really hard—cracked open her skull, left part of her brain on the road—the doctors thought they'd be able to save her life for a while, just that she'd have some permanent brain damage from the…you know, from the leaving part of her brain on the pavement—I guess you expect to not be all that all right when they're picking little pebbles out of your skull—but the surgeon who was in charge of putting her brain back together screwed up and she died on the operating table. My mom sued. The case was dismissed. We ended up with nothing. So, anyway, now I'm an only child—so…so there it is.

So there's life and there's death, you know? There's a legend…about a woman named Dierdre…well I mean, like we're Irish and everything, and Dierdre was supposedly the most beautiful woman on the whole island—

But anyway, she was so beautiful that people kept on fighting over her and killing each other in order to kidnap her. So finally this guy kills her true love and takes her away to be with him. But instead of being his wife, Dierdre kills herself by smashing her head on a rock repeatedly. I think about that.

About having the guts to be able to do that. I mean, to not just hit yourself once, but to do it again and again…and maybe that's what happened to my sister…maybe she had just had enough—of this place, of the ruin, of this slow crumble.

## ESL
by Tom Smith

Ofelia, a 16-year-old Mexican immigrant, explains how her life has changed since arriving in America.

**OFELIA:** We moved here when I was in seventh grade. The language wasn't the worst part, believe it or not. There's a whole cultural thing that's different. That's what was so weird. When I first moved here I couldn't believe how many clothes people owned. I mean, everyone had a closet just crammed full of stuff. We had to wear uniforms to school, so we only needed clothes for the weekend. But in some ways it's cool because no one looks down on you because of what you're wearing. There's a bunch of things that are different in Mexico. Like, in the afternoons everyone is outside playing, or watering their lawns, or whatever so you say "hi" and catch up on things. Here, everyone goes home and stays inside all day. And when I say "family," I mean all my aunts and uncles and cousins and grandparents; here, people just mean their immediate family. It's just all a little...different.

## LOCKDOWN (1)
by Julia Edwards

Alice is the quiet teenager who reads the dictionary. She and a bunch of classmates are in lockdown at school, and she recalls another time a year ago when there was a shooting.

**ALICE:** It was just a day. I guess you'd call it average. Like one of those days when you're complaining about how unfair the geometry final was and what a pain in the ass that kid Lance is and when you go home and your parents ask how school was, you just shrug your shoulders and turn on the television to watch some stupid rendition of teen life written by some burned out forty-something guy from LA. It was just...normal. And then you hear this noise. I would say gunfire but that's not what it sounds like because it's not like it sounds in the movies. And normal is turned inside out like one of those frogs in biology class. You don't know what's happening but you do know it's bad and you do know right then and there that it's going to take years to recover from this. You're like: this is traumatic. I'm experiencing trauma. And it races through your body like this terrible disease. Your heart is in your throat and you think you're going to choke to death if it beats again. And then you get this rush of adrenaline. Like those animals on National Geographic who suddenly realize that they're surrounded. Your legs start moving. You're running faster than you've ever run before. You don't even know where. You're doing this thing called saving your life and your brain is completely off-line. And all of a sudden there are these people there holding you and telling you it's over. They're shoving pamphlets in your hands about Why Bad Things Happen to Good People. And Where Was God? Your teachers and your parents and all the politicians are saying that you need to talk about this. And the only thing you want to do is watch that teen show written by the burned out LA guy and laugh at those evil cheerleader witches. But even he's sobered up and he's writing about trauma and violence and how to process pain. There's nowhere to go to escape it. Except in your head. So you decide to pass the time reading the dictionary and hope to hell that you'll feel better about life before you hit zyzzyra, but you always keep your running shoes handy just in case you hear the noise again. Just in case you have to run for your life.

## THE LOCKER NEXT 2 MINE (2)
by Jonathan Dorf

Habit, an outcast in her mid-teens, stands apart, not moving across the stage to help her friend Legolas, who has broken down after the entire contents of his locker have been painted black.

**HABIT:** I shouldn't be here. *(Beat.)* When my basketball coach died, back when I still played sports, back in sixth grade, I was the only player on the team who didn't go to the funeral. I had a piano lesson. My mom has the phone in her hand, and she's dialing my piano teacher, and I swear I almost grab it from her fingers. I didn't really do that, but I tell her no, I don't know if Mr. McCleary has any other times for my lesson. And my mom hangs up the phone, and that's that. *(Beat.)* And the day after the funeral, I hear them—all my teammates—talking about it and hugging, and I don't know what to say. I'm on the outside, and I will never again get back in. *(Beat.)* I want that night back. I want a do-over. I want to let my mom make that call. Maybe things would be different. Like in those movies when people go back in time, and they change one thing, and when they get home they live in a mansion instead of a one plus one apartment, and their parents are happy and never scream things like "I see how you look at her" or "you're such a bloodsucking bitch." I quit the piano six months later anyway. *(Beat. Pointing at Legolas:)* I should be there. But I just can't. I know if I take one step my insides will start to melt and my lungs will drown and I will end. I am not ready for the end of the world. Not yet.

## *An Actual Baby Person*
by Barbara Lindsay

Squishy is a very Goth, very pregnant teenager. Fearing she doesn't have what it takes to be a mother, she does her best to teach her irresponsible, good-hearted husband Dagger to fall in love with their unborn baby.

**SQUISHY:** Remember? You taught her how to talk. You taught her how to read before she even got to school. You used to brush her hair when it got all long and curly. Remember? You're the one who got her interested in chess. I got you a chess set for Christmas and the two of you learned together, so you were always a good match for each other. You helped her be smart, because you're the smartest person I ever knew. And you taught her how to give snappy answers to people who pick on her so they laugh and don't bother her any more. They always pick on the smart ones. Plus she's kinda small. But only at first. And then later she's gonna get long long legs and get really tall, and she starts wearing contact lenses, and every guy who sees her is going to think she's the most beautiful girl they ever saw. Everybody's going to call her Angel because she's beautiful, but she's also nice and sweet to everybody, but she's sincere about it, not, like, all fake and phony. She really means it. But you're her favorite. You and her have a really good friendship, right from the start. When she's a baby, sometimes she cries and cries and I can't do anything to make her stop, until I think I'm about ready to throw myself out the window. But then you pick her up and she right away starts smiling. That big baby smile with no teeth at first. And then one day, oh my gosh, there's just this tiny little bit of tooth poking through, and it hurts like crazy and she cries and drools all the time, but even so, when you pick her up, she gets this big smile all over her fat little face. She grabs hold of your finger, and her hands are so small, they don't even go all the way around. But she holds your finger tight, like she knows you'll always be there when she needs you, and you'll teach her everything she needs to know so she can grow up and be totally herself and totally independent and totally cool. Can you see her, Dagger?

## CHIRAPTOPHOBIA
by Hannah Estelle Sears

Teenaged Julia is at the funeral of a friend who died as a result of an eating disorder. She's alone with the coffin.

**JULIA:** I didn't want to speak at your funeral because there is nothing to say. You were sick and we all stood by, supporting you maybe but letting it happen too. Now we act like it was your time or there's some greater plan but we all know that the truth is we let you kill yourself. *(Getting fiery:)* I'm sick of dealing with eating disorders; half the people I know have them and it makes the world seem messed up and hopeless. I'm not going to let myself fall into the same trap as you, Rache. There are people dying everywhere because they don't think they're beautiful, don't think they're good enough, don't see anything worthwhile in the mirror unless they see a sliver of themselves. And it's not just appearances, no, it's control. Pressure has been mounting since we were little girls to be thinner, taller, tanner, smarter. You have to have a 4.0 and a slew of outside activities to get into any good college and on top of that you have to look like a model to have a social life at all. *(Riled up. Nearly screaming:)* I hate this society that messes with our brains and skews our priorities! I hate McDonald's, Urban Outfitters, politics and global warming. I hate diets and donuts and capitalism, I hate scales and coal and modern-day slavery! I hate California! Hollywood! I hate the models and runways and size double zeros! What the hell is that anyway? Double zero? Really?

## BETWEEN MARS AND ME
by Rose Helsinger

Jamie, in high school, has been looking after her paranoid older brother, Roland.

**TABATHA:** I lost you. *(Beat.)* My brother cast a long shadow. He beat me at chess in every game we played. He never let me win. He cared about his grades and shaved every morning at six am. He baked coffee cake with Mom and delivered pizzas to help us make ends meet. I love my brother. I miss him. I don't understand what happened or why I might never see him again. I look at you and I see a ghost of him. I look at you and I wait for him to come home.

*(Roland doesn't reply.)*

Say something.

*(Nothing.)*

I don't know what to do. I thought when I opened the curtains and you saw people, the world, that you'd get better. You stopped talking about aliens and I thought it was over. But it's not and I don't know what to do. I tried to step up. Take care of Mom like you did. Take care of you. But I'm not you. I'm not strong enough. I'm doing the best I can, but I'm fifteen. Tell me what to do. Tell me how to help you.

*(Roland remains silent.)*

Fine. I can't do this anymore. I'm leaving. I'm sorry. Here's your Christmas present. I picked it out. This one's from Mom. She sends her love.

*(Jaime walks to the door.)*

I'm not coming back.

## LOCKDOWN (2)
by Julia Edwards

Lily, a.k.a. Crazy Lily, is one of a group of teens trapped in the library when her school goes into lockdown. While rumors that she hears Satan circulate, there's more to her than meets the eye.

**LILY:** I know. Normally I do. Three shots a day since I was nine. I'm not complaining. Most of the time it's no big deal. It's just a fact of life. Like flossing your teeth. But sometimes...you just don't want to do it. And when your dentist asks you if you've been flossing every day, you say, "yeah," and he looks at your bleeding gums and knows you're lying. Same thing. Sometimes you get this craving for a dozen sour cream Krispy Kremes straight out of the fryer. But you just took your injection and if you had that much sugar—well, you just say you're not hungry. Or this guy, who doesn't totally nauseate you, in fact, he kind of makes you laugh, finally invites you to check out his band after school. You are so dying to go, your stomach is tied up in knots. But you know that you just used your last bottle of insulin, so you tell him "maybe some other time" even though you know he'll never ask again. Sometimes you just want to break the rules because you're only 17 once. You know it's not good for you, you know you shouldn't do it, but it shouldn't kill you.

# FEMALE OR MALE

## DEAR CHUCK (2)
by Jonathan Dorf

A teenage child of divorce reminisces about a now absent dad and the breakfasts they shared.

TEEN: When I was like six, my dad had an awesome job. I don't actually know what he did, but he was home having breakfast when I was having breakfast for school. He'd have bran cereal every day. He said it kept him regular. I thought that meant if he didn't have it his head would spin around and he'd puke green slime or something, so I was glad for the bran. I didn't want that to happen to me either—and I figure my dad knows what he's doing so I have it too. Only can we add some honey to mine, 'cause not turning into a monster doesn't taste as good as I was hoping. And I wake up 15 minutes early, 'cause my dad's reading the newspaper, and he reads the sports with me. We do this every morning until I'm in middle school.

(*Beat.*)

Yeah, I know your parents aren't cool, but it's not like people can see us.

(*Pause.*)

In seventh grade, my dad switches to Greek yogurt and fruit, because it's protein and low carb, and he drinks coffee but not fruit juice. I stick to bran, but if Dad's doing fruit, I'm doing fruit. Mostly bananas. Mom cuts them up and leaves them in a bowl covered with wax paper. She spends breakfast taking showers—she says this is father-son time—but as long as the fruit's in the bowl and I can just dump it on the bran, life is good. And when we finish, Dad goes into his study and Mom comes out of the shower and I go to school.

(*Beat.*)

But it gets harder when he moves to the other side of town. So breakfast turns into brunch, which is something that happens on Saturdays and Sundays.

(*Beat.*)

And then Dad gets a job three states away. This time, I know he designs buildings, and brunch becomes summer. But this year, there's music and tennis and tutoring for my SATs because my mom is freaking out that they're going to be too low. I don't think she's doing it on purpose, but I think I can only see him for a week this year.

(*Beat.*)

I'm glad the screaming matches and the silences that made me want to get up and run away are over, but a week of breakfasts...? I know I shouldn't—I know it's better for everybody—but part of me would trade a few more broken coffee mugs and an earful of words that made the stuff kids say at school seem like hugs and kisses for a few more breakfasts of bran and bananas.

## SNAKES IN A LUNCHBOX
by Arthur M. Jolly

Peyton, a middle school bully, has had a complete change of heart after witnessing violence at home.

**PEYTON:** Last night, my dad left the halfway house, came over and punched my mom in the face a bunch until she picked up a knife out of the sink and stuck it in his arm. Which is...he's okay. I mean, he's not dead or anything, but the way she looked when...he's gonna be in the hospital for a bit 'cause she hit an artery, and then he's going back inside. It's a violation of his condition of release or something, so there isn't even going to be a trial or nothing. The thing is...when she did it, I wasn't...I saw them fight, you know, before he—I mean, the first time. They fought a bunch, but she never...it was always them fighting. The two of them, it's how they were. Last night, I looked at her face—and I thought she was going to kill him. Stab him in the neck, or the heart. And I didn't feel bad about it. Not one bit. I just thought: took you long enough, Momma. *(Beat.)* Don't tell anyone. *(Beat.)* Never mind, say whatever. I figure everyone will know in a day or two anyway. They always do.

## *My Little Brother*
by Dan Berkowitz

A teen confesses to resenting the attention received by a special-needs younger brother.

**TEEN-AGED KID:** My little brother is the ugliest kid in the whole entire world. I mean it. Go to Wikipedia, enter the word "ugly," and there's a picture of my brother. He's, like, a foot shorter than me, but he weighs about a thousand pounds more. He wears big dorky glasses. His hair...looks like a dog was digging for a bone in it. He has lips that look like big globs of meat. A friend of mine once said they looked like liver lips. I started to call him "Liverlips" but my Mom told me to cut it out. He just smiled. He always smiles. Always. No matter what happens. I mean, how not-cool is that? And he drools. Makes me want to throw up.

He got this sweatshirt for Christmas two years ago? He took a marker and printed "King of the Dorks" on the front of it in big block letters. Seriously. See, when he first heard the word Dorks, he thought they were, like, some alien life form out of *Star Trek* and that they were, like, really smart? And he wouldn't change his mind, no matter how many times I tried to tell him that was lame. So then he decided he wanted to be King of the Dorks. I mean, how dorky is that? It's, like, dork squared. Cubed. No, it's dorkdom to the tenth power. Whatever that means. Of course, he misspelled "King" so the sweatshirt actually says "Kink of the Dorks," which is even more ridiculous. And he wears it everywhere, and it's falling apart, but he won't throw it away, and he's convinced that when people stare at him they're thinking he's the coolest kid around. I mean, really...?

# Go Solo

He always comes with Mom when she picks me up, or drives me anywhere. I've asked her a million zillion times not to bring him—especially when we're giving a ride to some of my friends—but she always says she has to bring him because she can't leave him alone and I should just deal with it.

But I've <u>been</u> dealing with it all my life. Well, since I was five, which is when he was born. It seems that no matter what I do, or how much I accomplish, <u>he</u> always has to come first, and the spotlight always has to be put on <u>him</u>.

Anyway, I don't know what's wrong this time, but I can tell Mom's been crying a lot. Of course, she says she hasn't. She says she's got allergies and they make her eyes water, but I know that's a crock. A couple of days ago, I overheard one of the doctors say it's a miracle he lived this long, and they should be grateful for the time they had with him, and they should "prepare themselves"—whatever that means. He's been really sick a couple of times before, but this seems, I don't know...different.

And there's a part of me that's thinking that if, this time, he doesn't make it, maybe we can just be a regular family, and maybe Mom and Dad won't always be so stressed out, and maybe we can do normal stuff like my friends' families do. And there's a part of me that's kind of...almost...a little bit...hoping for that. Y'know? But then I feel really bad, because while my brother is really a pain, he's, well, my brother. Y'know?

Sometimes life really sucks.

## *Dear Chuck (3)*
by Jonathan Dorf

A swim club. A teenager, perhaps holding a rubber ducky, a towel and whatever else would make him or her suitably dressed to go swimming, points at a lifeguard.

**TEEN:** I should totally get a lawyer and sue that guy. Sue him for every penny he's got, and sue the swim club, and I might just sue you too. Somebody's gonna' pay for my civil rights gettin' violated.

(*Pause.*)

Don't give me that look like you don't know what I'm talkin' about. Playin' dumb isn't gonna' keep me out of the kiddie pool. The sign doesn't even say "kiddie pool." It says "wading pool." I want to wade. I'm real big on wading. I wade at the beach. I wade in the pond near my house, even waded in the Dead Sea once, which is really hard 'cause all the salt makes you float. Who am I bothering if I wade here? I mean hey — I'm probably the only guy in there that wouldn't change the color of the water.

(*Pause.*)

The lifeguard says maybe if there's nobody else in the pool he'd let me swim. So I'm waiting. The kids from the summer camp are at the snack bar having their afternoon cookies and bug juice, so they're all getting out. But just as the camp kids are finally gone, there's this one little twerp — looks like he's two, maybe three — got those elbow flotation things, and he's crying his head off and his mom or nanny or housekeeper or whatever is draggin' him in. He obviously doesn't want to go — he's trying to bite her hand — so why doesn't this crazy lady just give the kid some time to get over it and stop scarring him for life. Because I don't want to see him turn into a psychopathic killer, and I don't own a bathtub, so this way, everybody gets what they want.

(*Pause.*)

What's her hurry? He's just hittin' the prime kiddie pool years. But I'm running out of time. I don't want to be goin' in there when I'm thirty — not that I shouldn't be allowed.

(*Pause.*)

I'm thinkin' about a petition. Or a boycott. Or maybe a march where everybody sings "We Shall Overcome." In a round. Because this is age discrimination, and it really sucks.

# Male

## ONE GOOD THING (2)
by Don Zolidis

Travis, 17, sweet, awkward, and a little bit bored, talks to the audience.

**TRAVIS:** Kimberly Lee Waluschka. To say that I was madly in love with her from a distance is something of an understatement because I lived next door—well, actually, she moved in about three months after we did—I already knew her, and I already had a crush on her, but when I found out she was moving in next to us, something snapped in my tiny little mind. I mean, it was like, suddenly I was obsessed. Suddenly I was making anagrams out of her name and counting the syllables to try to figure out if we destined for each other. I managed to sit behind her in American History, which pretty much consisted of me staring directly into her back and fantasizing about diving into a swimming pool filled with her hair. Homecoming. The dance. The important dance, and I knew she wasn't going out with anyone and here was my chance. I volunteered to mow their lawn, and I'd make sure to do it without my shirt on, and I'd do a whole bunch of push-ups before I went out there to make sure I was bulked up and everything, so when I mowed she'd see me and be so moved by my sunburned, scrawny physique that she would fall in love with me. Needless to say, that hadn't worked just yet. Sometimes I'd even go out there and throw a Frisbee to myself, you know toss it up in the air real high so she could see how athletic I was? That was...that hadn't quite succeeded yet either.

## LOVE (AWKWARDLY) (2)
by John Rotondo and Maryann Carolan

High school student Eddie is at his laptop looking at another student's Facebook page.

**EDDIE:** This is Wendy's Facebook. And it's not creepy that I look at it. I'm just interested in what she's doing. Okay, it is creepy. But I love looking at it. Makes me feel close to her when she's not there. See this pig? I gave her that pig on her birthday last year—when she was little, her mom called her Miss Piggy. *(He snorts like a pig:)* She's got 634 friends. Sometimes I friend her friends, even if I don't know them... Look at all these groups she belongs to. I never even knew there were this many different Sound of Music groups: The Sound of Music Fans three exclamation points; Dame Julie Andrews Rocks; Maria Von Trapp for Sainthood; Maria Von Trapp Is My Ideal Woman; Confidence and Edelweiss... I love her status updates. She's got great taste in music. Look: "Wendy McGann is gonna drive and never ever slow down". "Wendy McGann will write you visions of my summer— quoting lines from all those movies that we love." "Wendy McGann you're what keeps me believing this world's not gone dead, strength in my bones and the words in my head." Isn't that beautiful? Well...she didn't write it, but still, she wrote it in her status. Sometimes I think they're about me and maybe she's trying to tell me something through her status updates. Like they're secretly meant for me... Well, let's look at some pictures. Look at her profile picture—not one single picture taken in the bathroom mirror! Isn't that great? I like this one where she's upside down and all her silky shiny hair is hanging down. God, she's beautiful. Oh, look—Jessica tagged her in a photo. Eww— *(Reading the title of the photo album:)*

"There's A Party In My PANTS and Everyone's Invited!" God, Jessica's gross. Her friends are gross. I'm not against drinking, but these people spend 5 out of 7 days planning for it. Get a life, Jessica. *(He clicks on the photo:)* Huh. I didn't think Wendy was hanging out with these people. This was last weekend. I thought she had to go to Chuck E. Cheese.

*(He begins flipping through the pictures.)*

Oh. Umm. Yeah. This is...really sort of...you have to think...I...

*(Eddie closes his laptop violently.)*

I hate Facebook.

## *CREATURE FEATURES (MODERN DAY MUTANTS) (1)*
by Christian Kiley

When teen Cyrano is bullied by The Normals, instead of fighting back, he makes fun of his own nose. Cyrano's monologue is a modern day spin on the character Cyrano De Bergerac, who uses the same type of humor to thwart his enemies.

**CYRANO:** Before you attempt to rip me apart with your ridiculously predictable and far from scathing barbs, let me just say, in regards to my nose...it is like the facial version of the Leaning Tower of Pisa, an imperfect monument. When I get old and need help walking, I will be able to detach it and use it as a cane. When playing billiards, we will always have a cue! My face is a murder weapon twice, once in its ugliness to behold, and the second in the mortal wound that it can inflict with this dagger here. When I sniff, I destroy cities. I can rent out a nostril to store airplanes, cruise ships, and small countries. When Italy turns up missing, check my left nostril! The cost for the surgery to repair this monstrosity would mire me in lifelong debt. If you wanted to purchase my nose you would need to go through a real estate agent or perhaps two. It is a big deal! My sneezes are given names like hurricanes. Bears hibernate in my nostrils and sometimes they can't find their way out. I think there is also a litter of puppies up there. If my nose were floating in the ocean it could easily be an island. "Land ho, Australia!" And there is nothing that you have said or will say that shines any light on the issue.

## *HKFN: The Abbreviated Adventures of Huckleberry Finn*
by Jeff Goode

The teen actor playing Huck in a production of *The Adventures of Huckleberry Finn* is uncomfortable with the language in the play. It's rehearsal.

**HUCK:** *The Adventures of Huckleberry Finn,* also known as Huck Finn, by Mark Twain, also known as Samuel Clemens, American humorist 1835 to 1910. The end. *(Beat:)* Of the title, I mean. The play is just starting. *(Beat.)* I play Huck Finn. *(Opening the book:)* "You don't know about me without you have read a book by the name of *The Adventures of Tom Sawyer*. That book was made by Mr. Mark Twain, and he told the truth mainly, with some stretchers, but mainly he told the truth. I never seen anybody but lied, one time or another, without it was Aunt Polly, or maybe the Widow Douglas. Now the way that book winds up is: Tom and me found the money that the robbers hid in the cave and we got to keep it as a reward. The Widow Douglas adopted me and tried to bring me up proper. *(Rolls his eyes.)* From time to time, her sister Miss Watson would come stay with us. So then there was two of 'em. *(Sighs.)* And then Miss Watson took a set at me now with the spelling-book. She worked me middling hard till about suppertime and then they had to call in the—" *(To the director:)* I can't say this word. *(Substituting:)* "—the people. They had to call in the people from the fields to have supper and everybody went to bed." *(Explaining uncomfortably:)* You know... the people who worked for Miss Watson. *(Pointedly:)* For no pay. *(More pointedly:)* Because they were... *(Can't think of another word:)* people. Only that's not the word. It's another word for...people that I'm not comfortable saying in front of people. *(Resuming:)* "So after about a day of being educated and civilized, I was about ready to run off to the Territory and be a outlaw with Tom and his band of robbers. So later that night, Tom and me snuck off to plan our adventures, but when we got back home… Who did we see setting in the kitchen doorway, fast asleep, but Miss Watson's big… people…" *(Trails off…)* Than Jim. Than Miss Watson's big person Jim. *(Pointedly:)* Who works for her for no money and gets a switchin' when he does a bad job. And sometimes probably wishes he was free, but that's not gonna happen for another hundred years or so… *(To the Director:)* I'm sorry, I really can't say this word. And it's all over the place. It's practically the whole thing. And I really don't think we should be talking about it in school, should we? I mean, I know it's historical and that makes it okay. But I don't think that makes it okay, do you? I mean… *(Flips through the book.)* Nope, no, I can't. I'm sorry, I can't be in this show. I have to quit.

*(He walks out.)*

## THE BASEBALL KING
by Amelia Ross

Teenage David enters carrying a sign that reads, FREE COUNSELING WITH DAVID SHEPHERD. He never (ever) speaks. Phil Steen, the ultimate high school jock from a rival team, enters, making sure no one else sees.

**PHIL STEEN:** Hey David. Remember me? It's Phil Steen. *(Angry:)* The Giant you knocked out with a baseball! *(Beat.)* I shouldn't even be talking to you cuz, well, it's *you* I need to talk about. But no one else will listen. And I know you won't make fun of me if I tell you. You see, ever since you knocked me out with that baseball, everyone's been laughing at me. Kids used to hand me their lunch money in the cafeteria. They used to throw themselves against lockers when I walked down the hall, just so I wouldn't have to do it myself. But now, they call me sissy. They throw things at me. They, they...

*(David hands Phil Steen a card.)*

DON'T LET IT GET YOU DOWN. I don't need a pep talk. I want my dignity back. I wanna teach those losers a lesson.

*(David hands him another card.)*

GET IN A FIGHT. Closer. But I don't want to get my hands dirty.

*(David hands him another card.)*

TELL EVERYONE YOU BEAT ME UP. You'd really let me do that?

*(David nods.)*

Wow, David. You're the kindest, sweetest guy in the whole world.

## *XTIGONE* (2)
by Nambi E. Kelley

Le Roi, late teens or early 20s, has some very bad news for the powerful Marcellus—and he's really not eager to be the bearer of bad news.

**LE ROI:** Look, man.
I ain't gonna pretend I rushed to get here
'Cause, well...I didn't
Every time I thought about what I gotta say
I said, shoot, why I gotta be the one to tell?
And then I thought, shoot, if I don't tell
Marcellus
Gon' have my damn butt
On a platter
Splattered
With apple butter and coke
So I argues wit myself
"Self, what you gon' do?"
"Well, Self, I don't even be knowin'"
"Well, Self, if you don't tell Ol' Marcellus
He gon' kill your black butt
And you got kids to feed
And etcetera etcetera etcetera"
So Self said, "Shoot, I betta tell."
So here I be
I figure the worst that can happen
Is what already gon' happen
Cause "Everythang is Everythang" as Lauren Hill crooned
Once upon Duran Duran's "New Moon on Monday."

Listen Mack.
I ain't do it.

My name Bennet
I ain't in it.
My name Chuck
I don't know what up
Etcetera etcetera.
I ain't see who done did it, neither.
You know what I'm sayin' bruh?
And bad news be hard to tell
You know, Mack?
Somebody cleaned the dirt off Ol' dead E-Mem.
And threw the naked butt under the "EL" train tracks —

Whoever did it, who by the way I don't be knowin' who it was
Left no hint or sign.
No shovel
No bucket
Not even a spoon.
Just went away in the night
Like the Phantom of the Opera or some ish.
Then the morning guard showed it to us.
We got sckared, cause it lookeded like somebody tryin' to spook a spook
Like somebody was sckared if they didn't unearth Ol' E
There was gon' be some curse on the body
Or the family
Or some ish.
It was an unearthing down with sendin' some fool home to Spirit
Nah what I mean?
Then we, the guards, started accusin' each other, like, "It was you, man, wuzn't it?" "Naw, dude, it wuzn't me, it was the chubby chaser."

"Naw, man, it wuzn't me either, it was the funny lookin' one with the messed up fade." "Naw, it wuzn't me, man,"
I screamed
"Not my butt, I got kids to feed and etcetera etcetera etcetera"
Then one guard said
"Well, we gotta tell Boss-cellus"
We drew straws to see who would bring the news.
So here I be.
I ain't welcomed.
I don't wanna be here.
You remember that song from *The Wiz*?
"*DON'T NOBODY WANNA BE BRINGIN' NO BAD NEWS?*"
I brangs da truth.

## LAST RIGHT BEFORE THE VOID
by Jonathan Dorf

Christian, 17, hitchhiking on a deserted highway, talks to a woman who hitchhikes on the other side of the road and carries a sign that says "Alaska."

**CHRISTIAN:** Do I look like I killed my father and slept with my mother? *(Beat.)* Do I? *(Beat.)* I thought you might want to know. I'm hitchhiking because my car broke down. That's a lie. It broke down, but it's not my car. It's my father's car. Pieces of it broke off when I ran over my father in front of our house. That's a lie. He's not my real father. My real father killed himself when I was two. Or four. My mom tells it both ways. When I was two, he took me to a baseball game, then left me with a hot dog vendor and hung himself in a bathroom. When I was four, I was asleep and he stuck a shotgun in his mouth and woke me up from a dream about a seahorse. *(Christian crosses the road to the Woman:)* He also killed himself when I was six by jumping into a pool of concrete at a construction site or by suffocating himself in a plastic bag. I was at my grandparents' for the weekend. *(Beat.)* Do you really think someone's going to drive you from Minnesota to Alaska? *(Beat.)* I go to community college. I wish I could live at school. I don't think I'd have so many problems at home if I lived at school. That's a lie. I dropped out, because I got fired from my job at the mall. I handed out flyers for a seafood restaurant—Joe's Seafood—until I got fired. And I was in this Calvin Klein underwear ad when I was 12. With my shirt off. That's a lie. It wasn't Calvin Klein, and I was 16. I'm 19 now. *(Beat.)* I walked through an accident up the road. It's a big one. You'll see it if you go that way.

## Techies
by Don Goodrum

High school student Charlie Porter is the fragile star of *Jezebel's Last Chance* and has just found out that Bonnie, his long-time friend and co-star, is not going to make that night's performance. To make things worse, she is being replaced by Camille Curry, an unforgiving actress who has no patience with Charlie's sensitive nature.

**CHARLIE:** *(Almost hysterical, crosses to Tony and grabs him by the shoulders:)* Anthony, you have to help me! What am I going to do? Bonnie, my dear sweet Bonnie who would never hurt a fly has abandoned me, cast me aside like an old doll—! *My lines*, Anthony! You know how I am in a play, flying along one moment, focused with the razor-sharp intensity of a laser and then poof! One errant downdraft and I'm cast out of the nest, falling into a spiral of— Bonnie used to help me, Anthony! She knew that my mind could betray me like snow on a hot sidewalk, and so, with that phenomenal memory of hers, she would memorize my lines as well as her own and feed mine to me under her breath whenever tragedy would strike! Not that I would need it often, of course—but the idea of her, the security of her, waiting there, ready to lift me up and help me fly— *(He pauses as the horror of what he's up against sinks in again.)* But Camille Curry, Anthony! The Diva of Death! The Eater of Actors, who devours her fellow performers as if they were served on crackers with cheese…do you remember what she did to Will Hooper two years ago, in *As You Like It*? He went blank in the middle of a beautiful little soliloquy, but did Camille feed him a line? Did she help him find his way back on track? No. She just smiled. And waited for him. For. Ten. Minutes. She held everyone else off the stage by the sheer force of her Machiavellian will and just waited, *(Softer:)* watching as his psyche slowly crumbled, as his confidence broke down and his spark just...went...out. *(He sniffs loudly, on the verge of tears:)* Heartbroken and shattered, William never returned to the stage. I heard he was working at Chuck E. Cheese. *(Huge sob:)* As the squirrel... Anthony, don't let Camille eat my soul! Please! You have to save me!

## Two Dudes from Daytona
by Matt Buchanan

Lance, late teens or early 20s, is about to leave Florida and seek his fortune in New York. He speaks here with his dog, Crab, by his side.

**LANCE**: You know, I think my dog, Crab, is the most unsentimental beast on the face of the earth. When they heard I was moving to New York, the family almost lost it, man. My old lady was crying in her soup. My old man was punching walls and bawling. My sister was inconsolable. So was my brother, the little wuss. But not Crab. Dude, this dog never shed one single tear. Not one. I'll show you how it was:

*(Lance begins shedding clothing — nothing risqué — to illustrate his story.)*

This flip-flop is my father. No, wait, this one is my mother. No, that can't be right, man. Wait, it is right. Or left. This one has a hole in the sole, so this one is my mother. She never had much soul. This other flip-flop is my father. This belt is my sister. See how skinny she is? She never eats! This hat is my brother. He's always got to be on top of everything. Give himself apoplexy one of these days, man. I am the dog. No, wait...the dog is the dog. *(Pause.)* Then who am I? Oh! I am me, and he is him. Or he. Anyway...

*(He does an elaborate puppet show as he narrates.)*

Now, here's my old man. *(To the shoe:)* Pops, I'm moving up North. *(As the shoe:)* Oh, boo, hoo, hoo! Oh, no, not our boy! A day I hoped would never come! *(To audience:)* And here's my old lady. *(To the other shoe:)* Ma, I'm going to New York. *(As the shoe:)* Ahhh! Oh, noooooooo! Whatever will we do? *(To audience:)* And here's my sister. *(To the belt:)* Sis, I'm off to find my fortune. *(As the belt:)* No, you can't! I'll miss you so! Oh, boo, hoo, hoo! *(To audience:)* And my bro. *(To the hat:)* Bro, I'm done cleaning pools for a living. I'm off to the big city, man. *(As the hat:)* Oh, no! We love you so much! We need you! Don't go! *(To audience:)* And all this time, what does Crab do? He sits there. Not one word does he say, man! No feelings at all. Come on, you unfeeling cur.

## *The Ghost Moments (2)*
by Randy Wyatt

Matty, 20ish, has promised to try to exorcise a spirit from his sister's apartment.

**MATTY:** Hello?
Hello?
OK, awesome. Don't talk to me. Good plan. I really really like this plan. Just keep silent and we'll be juuuust fine.

*(He dumps out the contents of the bag — a couple sticks of incense, an incense holder, several books of matches, a wooden cross, a plastic bottle full of water, a smartphone.)*

Stupid Carly. I wouldn't even be here if she and her stupid stoner boyfriend OH MY GOD WHAT WAS THAT?!?

*(He listens intently. There's nothing.)*

OK. OK don't talk to me. OK? OK. I'm serious. I will completely lose my mind if you suddenly talk. Not funny, alright? All I'm here to do is cleanse this place of your demonic spirit, and then we can both go about our respective existences. You on your plane or whatever, and me on...mine.

God I hate this. I HATE this.

I mean, I bet it's no picnic for you either, being dead. And evil. And possibly not even existing at all but just being a figment of my sister's screwed up imagination while freaking herself out after she and her wastoid Chad—I mean seriously, CHAD...I know, right? I give it three months tops—they were up here drinking Jagershots until three watching spooky DVDs when Chaaaaaad gets this brilliant idea to make a Ouija board out of a pizza box and a Sharpie and suddenly bam! YOU and now they won't come back here until I...you know.

You didn't just breathe, did you? I heard breathing. I HEARD BREATHING. DO GHOSTS BREATHE?

OK. OK. It's me. It's me! I'm breathing. Which is good. I like breathing. You don't breathe. You're dead. OH MY GOD.

I don't even know if I'm doing this right. But OK, whatever. OK.

*(A pause. He straightens up and gets serious.)*

I hereby cast you out of this place by the power infused in me — wait. Infused? That's not right. That's like — iced tea. Invested? Invested in me by the state of...no, that's a wedding. It compels you to? Um. Huh. Something about compelling. You're compelled. So there. I probably should get my verbs right. STOP LAUGHING AT ME.

I'm serious. I'll come back here with a priest and a ghostbuster pack and a whole lot of garlic if I have to. CARLY IS NOT SPENDING ANOTHER NIGHT ON MY COUCH. JUST. GO.

*(A deep sigh.)*

She's my sister and I love her. She's my sister and I love her. She's my sister and murder is illegal.

THE INTERNET.

*(He pulls out his smartphone and fires it up. He speaks into it.)*

Exorcisms for people who might not believe in anything.

*(Looks at results.)*

Oooookaaaaay. I'm gonna be here awhile.

Step one: Acknowledge the existence of the ghost. Step two: Explain calmly and respectfully that its presence is no longer wanted there. Step three: Bid the spirit begone. Burn some fresh sage if necessary.

Well, I mean. When is that not necessary? Burnt sage.

Acknowledge the existence of the ghost.

Hi ghost. If you're actually there. What up? If I'm not talking to myself. Ugh. I don't think this is really acknowledging you.

Let's skip this step. I'll come back to it.

Step two. Calmly and respectfully.

Heyyyy there. I know you've probably had a rough time of it lately. It can't be easy, being you. I'm validating your feelings. I just want to take a moment and say, calmly and respectfully, get lost. No, wait no, that's not very. Respectful.

Please go away.

I mean, come on, it can't be very fun here for you. Isolating is never healthy. I know. I'm not exactly the social one. That's Carly. She's always the one pulling me into parties and meeting me for lunches and checking in on me and—

Do you have a sister? A sibling? I'm thinking you don't. Or you wouldn't be here. You'd go haunt them. That's actually kinda sad for you.

Did I just acknowledge you?

No. I still don't think you're there. Or maybe you are. You haven't tried to freeze my blood yet or anything, which I super appreciate, by the way. Can you even do that? Please, please don't answer.

Stupid Chad.

*(He sighs and gets comfortable.)*

I think it's gonna be a long night.

*(He keeps vigil.)*

## *CLAY (2)*
by Carol S. Lashof

High school sophomore Will is dealing with his changing perception of his own cultural identity.

**WILL:** I have this dream where I go back to my grade-school playground and I say to the other Black boys: Am I Black enough for you now? Am I? Black enough?

Kindergarten, first grade, second, third, it was always Sophie Janowitz and me at the top of the class and best friends. Math: when the other kids were doing drill-and-kill arithmetic problems, row after row, we got to sit in the hallway with a book of logic games, like figuring out if you told your parents you'd wash the dishes for just a penny on the first day and then double it every day—by the end of week three you'd be making more than $10,000. Sophie and me, we figured out by the time we were ten, we'd be billionaires. Then we got the giggles trying to decide how we'd spend all that money, and the teacher across the hall got mad about the noise and sent us back to our classroom and complained to Mr. Theodore about letting us be on our own in the hallway. But he kept on letting us anyway. He was chill. And he liked us, he trusted us—I could tell.

The third-grade spelling bee: down to the wire. Sophie spelled "orangutan." I spelled "CONNECT-I-CUT," remembering to say "capital C." We both messed up on "vivacious." She beat me on "rhythm."

This school is so big, if something gets screwed up, you can grow old and die trying to fix it. For instance, last year, in ninth grade, they put me in Algebra I instead of Algebra II— and by the time I got moved to the right class I was way behind and the teacher was pissed off about having to deal with me. He didn't think I belonged there—I could tell.

This year, my classes are mostly so boring I don't see the point of going. No one notices whether I'm there or not anyway. There's a computer that's supposed to call home when you're absent, but mostly I can erase the messages before my parents get home. My parents, they're always on me about college, college, college, like going to a good college is the only thing that could possibly count for anything ever. But they're not the ones who have to sit in those classrooms every day. They have no idea...

When I see Sophie with her friends, crossing the park on the way to school, or in the hallway between classes, she always waves and smiles but her friends, they look at me and they just see "scary."

I guess I'm Black enough for them.

## *The Grippe of October (1)*
by John P. McEneny

Clifford, pre-teens to early teens, has an intellectual disability. His mother is dying of the flu during the Spanish Flu pandemic after World War I.

**CLIFFORD:** My brother could swim the entire Hudson from Albany to Troy and then swim back with the outgoing tide. And he went to France. And rode in a submarine. And shot hundreds of Germans. And he kissed Florence Burt in back of the Empire Music Hall. And he could make my mother laugh even when there was nothing to laugh about. And he punched both the Clark boys in the face when they called me feeble. And he made—things—everything nice and bright. Every time he walked in the door, he was happy to walk in and see us. I can't sing. I can't sing the way it would make her happy. I can't do nothing to make her happy. I can't make her happy.

## RUMORS OF POLAR BEARS (1)
by Jonathan Dorf

Noah, 18, explains to Deme how he lost his family and found the group of (now) teenagers he travels with.

**NOAH:** I can't do much, as you can see. But that's one thing I'm good at. I've had the very best practice of all. *(Beat.)* I was playing piano. I used to take lessons three times a week from a woman with the whitest hair you've ever seen and a hand that would shake just a tiny bit, but in another life she'd played Carnegie Hall and been a soloist with every orchestra between Portland and Paris, and when she touched the piano the shake would vanish. I loved my lessons, and unlike almost any other seven-year-old on the planet, I loved to practice. I'd make my parents sit in the easy chairs by the window and play "concerts" for them. *(Beat.)* One time my mother got up in the middle of a movement of Tchaikovsky. I stopped and started banging on the keys like a maniac until she sat back down. And thus I trained my parents to stay until I played the very last note, and got up from my little booster bench. *(Beat.)* And on a beautiful April day, they are sitting there as I regale them with Mozart's Piano Concerto Number 15 in B-flat major, which would be extremely challenging at any age. They're still sitting there as we hear this far away thunder, and I look up from my Mozart and see the hint of a plume of distant dust through the window, but I don't stop playing, so they don't stop sitting, and they are still in their chairs when the entire side of the room by the windows falls away into nothing. I don't know what to do. A seven-year-old brain cannot process houses and parents winking into never agains, so I finish the 15th, but I am troubled by the middle C, which has gone terribly flat. *(Beat.)* I cry for half an hour—32 minutes, actually—but when it becomes clear that my piano is irrevocably broken, and that neither my parents nor the woman with the white hair will be coming back to listen to me play or for any other reason, I stop crying, close the cover, and two days later, I find *(Indicating the others:)* them. And we keep going. *(Beat.)* They're ready. *(Turning master of ceremonies:)* Mrs. Middleton's Former Pre-Kindergarten Drama Class Presents the Pageant of the Animals.

## CREATURE FEATURES (MODERN DAY MUTANTS) (2)
by Christian Kiley

Teen Charlie shares the story of how he played hide and seek as a child and no one looked for him. He shares this as a way of accepting his uniqueness and discovering his willingness to forgive.

**CHARLIE:** One time, when I was very little my big brother let me play hide and seek with his friends. It was a thrill. It was the big leagues of hide-and-seek...in a small forest next to our house. No way was I going to be the first one found, so I went to the deepest part of the forest and hid. I had to control my giggling. It was such a great spot. And I waited and waited and waited. The most patience any kid has ever shown, ever. And it started to get dark and then...it got dark. And my face got hot and...why would they not look for me? Not one of them. I made a makeshift bed under some leaves and slept there. It got pretty cold and the sounds were frightening. I mean it wasn't a real forest, it was one of those little park-forests that developers make to give you the sense that they didn't kill all of nature, just most of it. When I came home Saturday morning the breakfast dishes had already been cleared. Blueberry pancakes, my favorite, and not one left. I think I intentionally left some leaves in my hair to see if anyone would notice. They didn't. My heart is my ability to forgive.

## Exposure
by Vishesh Abeyratne

Patrick, 21, tells a story about the first time he got drunk, after his sister has had a bad experience as a result of a mistake of her own.

**PATRICK:** Okay...it was back in senior high. Also at a party. I'd had a few beers, so I was pretty far gone. My friends and I were singing really badly, goofing around and just acting like a bunch of idiots. And there was this park just down the road from the house where we were. It was late, so we decided to go out there and play a drunk game of "Sandman." So we got there and we were just about to head onto the playground when all of a sudden we saw this random couple on a bench. They were making out. And in my questionable state of mind, I thought this was hysterical. And that's when I got the bright idea to go up to those two and scare the living crap out of them. I went right up to their bench and knelt down next to them. And I cupped my hands to my mouth and went right up to the guy's ear. And I SCREAMED at the top of my lungs, I screamed, "GET A ROOM!!" They must have jumped about five feet in the air. The guy got really mad. He started yelling at me, then all my other friends. He started using all these slurs and threatened to beat us up. His girlfriend was trying to calm him down, but he was really freaking out. Then he started to push me. So I walked right up to the guy and started yelling at him. Called him a jerk for threatening a bunch of kids. Which, let's face it, he was. He looked at least 10 years older than us and he was bigger than me. *(Beat.)* Anyway, then he punched me. Right in the face.

We ran. We weren't completely stupid. *(Beat.)* Well, I was. They had to pull me away. Then we bolted. We didn't stop until we got back into the house and locked the door. Then I...puked all over the rug and passed out.

## ONE GOOD THING (3)
by Don Zolidis

Travis, 17, speaks to the audience about the death of his brother in Iraq.

**TRAVIS:** The sun was going down when I got outside. And I thought about what Nick had said to me, all that stuff about finding my place in the world, or finding some way to make a mark, and I hadn't done any of it. I hadn't made a single mark. Even at the funeral I wasn't all that important—not that many people really paid much attention to me. And it occurred to me that all I was really, was just a hole. Just an empty spot. And then I thought, I can't even believe that all I'm thinking about right now is myself. Maybe that's why I'm nothing. The whole world just goes on around me—my mom and dad are in there, hashing it out, my brother's in the ground, and I'm out here whining about the fact that I'm uncool. If I was really a good person, I'd be crying about Nick, but I'm not. I was the last person to talk to him, he even told me he was worried, in his way, and I remember during that conversation that I wanted to cut it short cause there was a good TV program coming on.

## Sunset Johnson
by Ed Shockley

Sunset, late teens to early 20s and a black soldier just back from WWI, has come upon Lila, a white girl who used to watch him secretly from afar, and an innocent flirtation has developed—one that could have dangerous consequences in the Jim Crow South.

**SUNSET:** I done picked a great big willow tree got leaves hang down almost to the ground. When you get up in there it be dark like night and cool as a creek side. I done found that spot and said to myself, this here is made for thrill. That willow done bowed down its head asking to see some loving. Every girl got a spot. Some are pretty like a twilight boat floating down the James River. Some are dangerous like a back porch or her husband's car. Sunset's always searching for the spot. Sometimes I find the girl first, another time the place. When I get them both together then we got us a good time. This willow spot, this is magical. It's made by God out here in the wilderness. And man and woman get in a spot like that then something's gonna come down on them. You already seen what's in these pants and you spozed to think that a man been half way round the world would know how to use it. Now, if he found him a special place where nobody know and he willing to risk lynching for one turn with you then you got to figure some special love about to fall. Can't nobody never know but you and him so the question on this hot summer afternoon is, "Do you want loving worth dying for?" Me, I'm heading out in the woods a quarter mile and relaxing under that cool willow off to the left of the path about 40 feet. I'm gonna walk slow cause that's how Sunset like to come. If 'fore long, a pretty girl were to happen along then we goan make ourselves a secret. You take care of yourself Delilah.

## RUMORS OF POLAR BEARS (2)
by Jonathan Dorf

Romulus, 15, surviving in the aftermath of a climate induced catastrophe, travels with his older sister and another teenage survivor. He feels guilt over not having gone with Cassie, a girl he met along the way.

**ROMULUS:** I lost track of how long we've been walking. Every day it's the same. Walk until it blazes high, hide until it starts to slide, walk until it sinks and dies. My feet turned rock, and I don't cry at night anymore. The water we took instead of the coloring book's almost gone, so I don't want to waste it outta my eyes. *(Beat.)* Deme says we're almost there. Maybe one more day. She says that every day. *(Beat.)* Yesterday, there was this lake. The biggest most beautiful lake I've ever seen. Hundreds'a feet around. *(Beat.)* It's almost empty really. If you laid on your back in the middle, it wouldn't even touch your face. *(Beat.)* I just want to wash it off. All the dirt that's stuck on me. And the water isn't deep enough. Maybe if it was deeper I could drown all the wrong and the bad and everything I've done and burst outta the water clean. But it won't come off. No matter how much I rub, it's just caked on me. Like a second skin I can't shed.

## WHAT HAPPENED AT THE MUD PUDDLE (3)
by Tara Meddaugh

Tom, middle or early high school, is at an extravagant yacht party of a classmate he barely knows.

**TOM:** I don't know why I was there. On some boat. With young men dressed in old clothes. Singing. Hitting the drums and playing the electric guitar. I'm not interested in that. I don't know Taylor. I don't know any of them. She gives us these $50 gift cards to the mall but the Best Buy closed down two years ago and there's not even an Apple store there yet. So what am I supposed to do with this gift card? My mom says we'll buy clothes. But I don't buy clothes at the mall. That's for girls. *(Pause.)* There is a CVS there though, so maybe I'll buy some candy. Starbursts. *(Pause.)* Maybe some cough drops. I usually get a few colds per season. I find coughing annoying. It wakes me up when I'm sleeping. But my mom won't let me suck on a cough drop in bed. So. *(Pause.)* I do it anyway. I'm not five. I can suck on a cough drop in bed.

## LOVE (AWKWARDLY) (3)
by John Rotondo and Maryann Carolan

Randy, a high school junior, has been kissing Laura—not his girlfriend—on a bench in the park.

**RANDY:** Look. I know what you're thinking. But I'm not that guy. This isn't who I really am. I know this looks bad. *(He looks at Laura:)* Really bad. I didn't mean for it to happen... This... Us. It just...did. Anything I say to you is going to make me seem superficial and shallow. Sometimes I think I am. A lot of times I think I don't deserve this. Okay, okay—I know I don't deserve it. I'm a schmuck. A user. A coward. I keep pretending like I can do this and no one will ever get hurt. Some sick and twisted part of me truly believes that if we could all be honest and open with how we feel that everyone would be much happier. Why can't I love two people? Why do I have to choose? Isn't there enough love in me to go around? There is. I know there is. I feel so guilty. You'd think my guilt would destroy my passion, wouldn't you? Trust me—it doesn't. She's so hot. No, not like that. That makes me sound like a real superficial jerk. I know what you're thinking, "That's right—he's a real superficial jerk." I am. I'm not. There's feelings inside of me that I can't label. Maybe I'm emotionally retarded. Maybe I'm afraid. But I want to be with both of them. And not together. Like I could cut myself in two—one half with Charlotte and one with Laura. I know you think I'm a jerk and a horrible human being. But this isn't me. This has become my idea of normal: sneaking around, deleting my texts as soon as they come in. Last week Charlotte went to grab my phone—she was just fooling around. But I knew there were a bunch of texts from Laura. And they were...uh...pretty incriminating. Charlotte kept going after my phone. I didn't want her to see it, didn't want her to find out that way. So I dropped it in the sink. My new $200 phone, floating in a bowl of soapy water because I'm such a coward. But you know the worst part? I was so mad at myself for everything, so pissed at my stupidity, that I let Charlotte believe it was her fault. She was so upset she gave me half the money for it. What am I supposed to do with that? There's $100 sitting in my sock drawer. How can I spend it?

## Platform Nine
by Rebecca Moretti

Sonny, a troubled but charming 16-year-old, has struck up a conversation with a girl as they share a bench in a train station, both of them running away from home.

**SONNY:** Well, I had one when I was a kid. A little goldfish. My dad got it for me for my birthday.

*(Sonny looks at Adelie to see if she is listening and she turns away.)*

I don't know why, but I loved that fish. I'd watch him a lot you know, swim around his little glass bowl. He really seemed depressed all the time. I mean, he didn't ever really have a lot of energy or anything.

*(He looks at Adelie, who is reading her book.)*

And so one day, I decided I'd set him free. I knew I'd miss him and all, but I just couldn't stand him being holed up in that stupid bowl all the time. So I took him down to the beach one day, and walked into the water as far as I could, while still holding the bowl. Then I just tossed him in there and watched him swim around... Man, I can't remember a time since I've felt that happy—you know, watching him swim around free in the ocean... After a moment, though, I saw he wasn't swimming anymore. His little body was just floating there on the waves...

## THE GRIPPE OF OCTOBER (2)
by John P. McEneny

Jack, 18, is a soldier in World War I suffering from influenza. Here he's writing to his mother.

**JACK:** Dear Mother, Sorry I haven't written. Please excuse my penmanship. They're calling it nerve exhaustion. As you might imagine, I'm all kinds of knocked about. But I'm not really as hurt as the doctors might have you believe. The legs have healed up really nicely and I can almost bend my knees. It takes a great deal to write so I won't be too loquacious. I fear you'll be unable to recognize me when I get back, Mother. I have seen so much that my very soul has been changed. I have always strived to earn your love and pride, but when I return, I shall be a much quieter person. A man you might not recognize. And I hope that you will find it in your heart to have the patience to love this new half man. I dream often of you playing baseball with Hal and me in the backyard, and you and Alice dancing in the parlor. Is that what we fought for? Tell them I am in good spirits and eager to return home. I am not as the Germans would have wished—"Kaput." Such a funny word: Kaput. I'll be in Albany soon. Much love, your son, Jack.

## *WAR OF THE BUTTONS (1)*
by Jonathan Dorf

Teenaged Siggy, who escaped from Bosnia (or wherever is suitable), tells the story of his escape in a moment out of real time as he and his American friends prepare to go on a "raid" against their rivals from the local prep school.

**SIGGY:** When the war happened, they came through the village, and if the people already killed had anything worth money, the soldiers would take it. They'd strip the bodies. The men and boys that were alive they'd bring together, and in some villages shoot them. That's what we heard from people running from the army, people who came through our village. Naked dead bodies, clothes in a pile. *(Beat.)* When we found out the soldiers were coming, my father told me take off all my clothes and put them in a pile. He and some of the other men did the same, and my mother and the other women told the soldiers that their army had already been through. *(Beat.)* We thought if they saw the bodies with no clothes, they'd think we were dead and they wouldn't bother with us. I had my eyes open, like I died with my eyes open, because it was the only way I could see if they were looking at me. To breathe. I tried to hold my breath, and when I had to breathe, only do it when I was sure nobody was looking. *(Beat.)* My father—something, a butterfly—landed under his nose. He sneezed. A soldier thought he wasn't quite dead and put a bullet in his head. A butterfly killed my father. And my mother tried not to, but she got so...so much crying, that they shot her. I laid—lied—lied there naked until the soldiers left. *(Beat.)* In a month, they snuck me out.

>*(Siggy finds some salt in his pants pocket and throws it over his shoulder.)*

Being naked...it's like being quiet...it makes you invisible...it makes you safe.

## WARRIORS (2)
by Hayley Lawson-Smith

Peter, in his final year of high school, has been given an essay to write as a disciplinary action; he beat up the boys who were bullying his little sister. Words in [brackets] indicate American substitutes for the Australian words.

**PETER:** April, 2014. I'm supposed to be writing a report; how to solve issues in a diplomatic, non-violent way. If I don't write this stupid report, I won't be able to play footy [football] this season. I don't care. They'll lose without me, but Dad says that's a small price to pay for defending your sister. Mom says at least now I'll have more time to study. I hope the guys on the team feel the same way. *(Pause.)* I'm going to write their stupid report. But I'm going to do it my way. *(Sarcastic. Writing:)* How to solve issues in a diplomatic, non-violent way. Step one: Live in an alternate universe where there are no arseholes [assholes/jerks]. Step two: Should disagreements arise, rely on the services of "magic fairies" to solve all your problems. Step three: If steps one and two are impossible, because they most likely *are*, and arseholes [assholes/jerks] bully your little sister, find them in the lunch break and sort them out [take care of them]. From then on, there should be peace and non-violence in the land of the playground. Step four: Being banned from footy [football] for the rest of the year, wait for the cricket [baseball] season to begin.

## HERBY ALICE COUNTS DOWN TO YESTERDAY (2)
by Nicole B. Adkins

Herby Alice, early to mid-teens, isn't the most popular kid at school, but he's a science genius. He's talking to aspiring reporter Rose, same age.

**HERBY:** Some nights when I can't sleep I carry my telescope outside to my tree house. I spend hours...just looking into space. And you know something? As long as I stay, I never see any more than the smallest portion of what's out there. *(Beat.)* Rose, I'm sorry I pressured you about helping me. We're on different paths now. I understand that. I guess...I just—miss the way it was, you know, when we were kids? Last year? You've always been my best friend. But now...well, I guess you're pretty busy with the media circus. You've got your new friends. Your extracurricular activities. Your new—look. *(Beat.)* You were never invisible to me. *(Beat.)* You'll be great at broadcasting. Just like you are at everything. And I won't tell anybody that you still get straight As in science and math.

## *The Locker Next 2 Mine (3)*
by Jonathan Dorf

Legolas, a sensitive Goth teen, is in a classroom where they've just received the results of aptitude tests that they took earlier in the year.

**LEGOLAS:** Six years ago, my uncle moved from apartment 208 to apartment 103. Same building. And so they start sending his disability checks to 103, which is what you expect, right? And then suddenly 2 months ago they start going back to 208. Lucky it's in the same building, but what's up with that? *(Beat.)* People think I'm weird. I'm OK with that. Tiny Tim, the little gimpy kid from *Christmas Carol*, says maybe people will see him and feel better 'cause they're not him. I think I'm something like that kind of weird. But not crazy. Not like "we flew our own planes into the Towers" crazy. And I say that the check suddenly going to my uncle's old address, or Jeremy's old aptitude test coming back, that's not an accident. *(Beat.)* I just hope—I hope it makes things better.

## LONG JOAN SILVER
by Arthur M. Jolly

Jim is a young teenager, defiantly facing a gang of women pirates that he knows plan to kill him.

**JIM:** *(To all of them:)* I am not such a fool but I know what will happen in your company. I've seen too many die already. But there's a thing or two I have to tell you first. You're in a bad way—ship lost, treasure lost, crew lost, your whole business gone to wreck; and if you want to know who did it—it was I! I was in the apple barrel the night we sighted land, and I heard you, Joan, and you, Anne Bonney, and Hands, who is now dead and gone, and I told every word you said before the hour was out. As for the schooner, it was I who cut her cable, it was I that killed Israel Hands aboard of her, and it was I who brought her where you'll never see her more, not one of you. Kill me if you will, for it's all you know. I will not join you. *(Pause.)* When they kill me, Joan Silver—I'll take it kind of you to let the doctor know the way I took it.

## *WAR OF THE BUTTONS* (2)
by Jonathan Dorf

Ticker, 12, a hyperactive imp who has just gotten into a fight with some students from the nearby prep school, talks to Charlie, 15. Charlie's parents have left him—and it's starting to look as if it's for good. They're on a sidewalk, where Charlie sits with his family's luggage.

**TICKER:** I'll stay with ya'. *(Beat.)* You gonna eat that cone? I was over at Gene's for lunch, and it's like just 'cause his Mom's my aunt she thinks she's gotta feed me all these vegetables.

> *(Beat, then Charlie gives it to him. Ticker takes a bite, then continues to eat as he talks. As Ticker talks, the lights should dim almost imperceptibly as it grows later.)*

My Mom said I could get these new pump sneakers. She found this mail order place that sells 'em for ten bucks less than K-Mart.

> *(Charlie nods distractedly.)*

If I come up with 20 from my paper route, she'll gimme the other half.

> *(Ticker takes off one of his worn sneaks.)*

Need 'em bad. See?

> *(He removes a piece of colored construction paper from inside the shoe; it covers a hole in the sole. He shows Charlie.)*

Stole 10 sheets of construction paper off the art teacher's desk. Good as new. Rubs somethin' bad though. *(Beat.)* I gotta get home or I won't get dinner. She says if I miss again I'm not eatin'. Period. And when she says period... You wanna come for dinner? There probably isn't any extra, but I'll give you some 'a mine. *(Beat.)* If they don't, and you want somethin' to eat, just throw stones at my window like on TV. I'll save some 'a my dinner for ya', just in case.

*(Ticker drifts toward the exit.)*

You'll be at the factory tomorrow—right? 'Cause they're gonna' beat the hell outta' me if you don't come.

## SECRET LIFE UNDER THE STAIRS (2)
by Kris Knutsen

Bizzy, 11, a "not very much talking run up and karate chop you in the face" boy, pulls out a faded photograph from his pocket. He talks to it when he thinks no one is watching. He doesn't know that his friend Lu, a year younger, hides nearby.

**BIZZY:** I found a moment I lost from yesterday. It was lying on the floor and a sunbeam led the way and I stepped back into the day before my mother went away. *(Beat.)* Standing in the beam I touched the feeling of your hair—how it softly scratched my face. I could smell that hand lotion on my t-shirts when you folded my clothes. I tasted the grey of your eyes as we sat down at the kitchen table and I heard the red plastic bowls filled with cereal as we watched cartoons together before school which made the time go by so fast. *(Beat.)* And then the flash of remembering faded and you faded in my hand and all I'm always left with is a fragment of a picture, and heavy feet on a floor with the present sight of nothing as you're not here no more.

*(Lu stands quietly, allowing herself to be seen. Bizzy turns, putting the photograph in his pocket.)*

What are you still doing here?

## *WARRIORS (3)*
by Hayley Lawson-Smith

Peter, in his final year of high school, is pondering yet another ridiculous essay question. Words in [brackets] indicate American substitutes for the Australian words.

**PETER:** A hard thing about growing up...a hard thing about growing up is...actually, I don't think it is hard to grow up, is it? I mean, it's not as though you have any choice in the matter. No, I think it's harder for the people around you to watch you grow up. Mom still thinks I should call her every hour — she still thinks I need her to drive me to the movies. She still thinks the parties I go to should have "adult supervision." Until a month ago, she still called me Peter Pan. It was all right to be called that when I was little, but she reckoned I should keep putting on green tights for every dress-up party I'm invited to. My little sister has only just now stopped calling herself Tinker Bell and making me help her fly around the room. Her first day of high school [junior high/middle school] she wanted to follow me around, calling me Peter effing Pan...I pretended she was someone else's sister. Mom doesn't call me Peter Pan anymore. She stopped when I yelled at her. Never yelled at my Mom about anything before, I thought Dad was going to lose it. But he kinda understood, so now Mom just calls me Peter or Pete. Growing up means your Mom shouldn't baby you; I don't reckon they'd let a guy nicknamed Peter Pan play in the Ashes [World Series].

## *Rumors of Polar Bears (3)*
by Jonathan Dorf

Romulus, 15, one of several teens surviving in the aftermath of a climate induced catastrophe, keeps watch as the others settle down to sleep. Once he's sure they're asleep, he pulls out a ratty book.

**ROMULUS:** I found this book. We're going through a squat like we do when we find one that's got nobody in it, which is always. Water food weapons power coin clothes fun and games, always in that order. Stick to the order—it might save your life. And this squat—no, this *house*—is so beautiful I want to live in it forever. They got windows like you wouldn't believe, and a pool that makes the party pool look like a bucket. No, like a puddle. Only the water's gone of course. And they got a giant bed and an almost giant bed and then just a really big bed—they got so many beds you could sleep in a different bed every day for a week. And if I could just get one night in even the really big bed, but Deme says the big dead is right behind and gotta keep moving. So I'm grabbin' everything I can, everything I can fit in every pocket, and I open a door and it's a library. A library. With books. Fancy books with fancy covers and gold and silver writing. *(Beat.)* Water food weapons power coin clothes fun and games. Don't jump the order. No way does a book beat a can of tuna. No way does a book beat a can of anything. I can hear Deme screamin' at me in my head. And I look at all the gold and silver books and I know they're too big and let me just leave now before I— It's so thin and the corner of the cover is folded over, but the cover has these two tiny people and this tree that looks dead and a whole lotta empty, and I just gotta have it, cause it looks like us. *(Beat.)* I read it when Deme's gone. I've read it 17 times. Except for the end. Somebody ripped out the last three pages. So I don't know if the man comes or not. *(From the play:)* Nothing to be done. *(Beat.)* I was two when Dad came home from the play, but I still remember. And when I do the play, I feel him watching. I know it's not his face I see, but it's my make-believe dad's face, and he's smiling.

## About YouthPLAYS

YouthPLAYS (www.youthplays.com) is a publisher of award-winning professional dramatists and talented new discoveries, each with an original theatrical voice, and all dedicated to expanding the vocabulary of theatre for young actors and audiences. On our website you'll find one-act and full-length plays and musicals for teen and pre-teen (and even college) actors, as well as duets and monologues for competition. Many of our authors' works have been widely produced at high schools and middle schools, youth theatres and other TYA companies, both amateur and professional, as well as at elementary schools, camps, churches and other institutions serving young audiences and/or actors worldwide. Most are intended for performance by young people, while some are intended for adult actors performing for young audiences.

YouthPLAYS was co-founded by professional playwrights Jonathan Dorf and Ed Shockley. It began merely as an additional outlet to market their own works, which included a substantial body of award-winning published and unpublished plays and musicals. Those interested in their published plays were directed to the respective publishers' websites, and unpublished plays were made available in electronic form. But when they saw the desperate need for material for young actors and audiences—coupled with their experience that numerous quality plays for young people weren't finding a home—they made the decision to represent the work of other playwrights as well. Dozens and dozens of authors are now members of the YouthPLAYS family, with scripts available both electronically and in traditional acting editions. We continue to grow as we look for exciting and challenging plays and musicals for young actors and audiences.

# About ProduceaPlay.com

Let's put up a play! Great idea! But producing a play takes time, energy and knowledge. While finding the necessary time and energy is up to you, ProduceaPlay.com is a website designed to assist you with that third element: knowledge.

Created by YouthPLAYS' co-founders, Jonathan Dorf and Ed Shockley, ProduceaPlay.com serves as a resource for producers at all levels as it addresses the many facets of production. As Dorf and Shockley speak from their years of experience (as playwrights, producers, directors and more), they are joined by a group of award-winning theatre professionals and experienced teachers from the world of academic theatre, all making their expertise available for free in the hope of helping this and future generations of producers, whether it's at the school or university level, or in community or professional theatres.

The site is organized into a series of major topics, each of which has its own page that delves into the subject in detail, offering suggestions and links for further information. For example, Publicity covers everything from Publicizing Auditions to How to Use Social Media to Posters to whether it's worth hiring a publicist. Casting details Where to Find the Actors, How to Evaluate a Resume, Callbacks and even Dealing with Problem Actors. You'll find guidance on your Production Timeline, The Theater Space, Picking a Play, Budget, Contracts, Rehearsing the Play, The Program, House Management, Backstage, and many other important subjects.

The site is constantly under construction, so visit often for the latest insights on play producing, and let it help make your play production dreams a reality.

# More from YouthPLAYS

*Directing Kids* by Matt Buchanan

Directing the school play for the first time? Or maybe you're an experienced hand always looking for ways to improve. Anyone who wants to help young casts create memorable theatrical experiences for themselves and their audiences will benefit from **Directing Kids**. With topics that range from choosing a play to blocking and actor coaching to dealing with parents and everything in between—presented in clear, step-by-step chapters—it's a comprehensive guide to directing and producing plays with young people.

**HKFN:** *The Abbreviated Adventures of Huckleberry Finn* by Jeff Goode
Comedy. 25-35 minutes. 3-8 females, 2-6 males (5-10 performers possible).

The actor playing Huck runs away from a production of Twain's controversial classic, **The Adventures of Huckleberry Finn**. But when the actor who plays Jim runs away too and troublemakers Duke & King join in, their fugitive theatre company launches into a series of misadventures—while the domineering Aunt Polly tries to force them back into the "real" play. In the chaos, that play—and its discussion about race—may be happening without them knowing it.

*Warriors* by Hayley Lawson-Smith
Drama. 40-50 minutes. 4 females, 1 male.

Not every hero gets a song or the cheers of the crowd—or even acknowledge. In Zordana's land, a hero fights in the open field, destroying monsters and dark magic. In Amy's world, her hero is the sister who takes care of her. For Maddie, her hero is her brother, who teases her mercilessly but loves her dearly. As tragedy threatens to consume their separate worlds, only in coming together can they battle back the dark.

## *Dream House: A Rainy Day Play* by Jeremy Gable
Comedy. 60-70 minutes. 1 female.

Jenn, a grown-up with a grown-up job, returns to the old rowhome in which she grew up. As a child, her father's hot air balloon accident forced her to stay with her super-paranoid Aunt Greta. Now Jenn has inherited the house, and with it a whole host of not-very-pleasant memories. With a thunderstorm approaching, Jenn must learn to reconnect with her childhood self, and use her imagination (along with an assortment of household items) to fight her grown-up fears. What follows is a menagerie of paint, puppetry, mime, song, and the notion of what it actually means to grow up.

## *The Locker Next 2 Mine* by Jonathan Dorf
Dramedy. 80-85 minutes. 5-12+ males, 8-16+ females (14-40 performers possible).

Alisa arrives at a new high school in the middle of the year to find her locker next to a shrine for a popular lacrosse player who's died in an auto accident, but as she digs deeper, she discovers another death that no one talks about, even as it's left many of the school's students trying to pick up their own pieces. A play about teen suicide and dealing with loss.

## *The Matsuyama Mirror* by Velina Hasu Houston
Drama. 60-70 minutes. 4 females, 1 male, 3 either.

In Matsuyama, Japan in the 1600s, a world before the discovery of mirrors, young Aiko comes of age in the aftermath of her mother's death. Gifted with a "magic" mirror, she sees her image and believes that it is her mother's spirit—and when her father remarries and she begins to grow up, Aiko resists, escaping into an enchanted world where dolls come to life. As they encourage her to stay to play and frolic, will Aiko fall into the fantasy forever, or will she discover the true magic of life?

### *Love (Awkwardly)* by John Rotondo & Maryann Carolan
Comedy. 35-40 minutes. 4 males, 4 females, 3-6 either (8-14 performers possible). Also available in a full-length version.

Eddie is hopelessly in love with his best friend, Wendy, who is infatuated with another guy. Luke and Roxanne seem perfect together, but she's about to graduate and leave him behind. Randy and Charlotte's relationship is…well, Randy's cheating on her with her best friend, Laura. Last year, Laura broke up with George, who still hopes desperately that she'll come back. *Love (Awkwardly)* follows these eight juniors and seniors through wonder, pain and exhilaration that are adult in magnitude but cramped by the confines of high school.

### *The Exceptional Childhood Center* by Dylan Schifrin
Comedy. 25-35 minutes. 2-4 females, 2-3 males (5-6 performers possible).

Reggie Watson has been accepted into the right preschool. He's set for life…as long as he can make it through the one-day trial period. But when desperation breeds disaster and his future hangs in the balance, Reggie and his band of quirky classmates may just discover things about themselves that school could never teach them.

### *Xtigone* by Nambi E. Kelley
Drama. 90-100 minutes. 5-15+ females, 4-15+ males (9-30+ performers possible).

Chicago. Present day. Xtigone's brothers have been killed in drive-by shootings by each other's rival gang. Her powerful uncle calls for the bodies to be buried instead of uncovering the violence in the city streets. In this re-imagining of Sophocles' *Antigone* that uses poetry, dance and dialogue that speak with an urban voice, will Xtigone go against his edict and risk death in her quest for her community's truth?

Made in the USA
Middletown, DE
20 November 2018